Listening to Youth

Listening to Youth

THE VIEWS OF IRISH YOUTH ON THEIR RELIGION

Bernadette MacMahon DC

DOMINICAN PUBLICATIONS

First published (1987) by
Dominican Publications
St Saviour's, Dublin 1

ISBN 0-907271-77-4

Cover design by Eddie McManus

Printed in Ireland by
The Leinster Leader Ltd.

Contents

Acknowledgements

This book is a follow-up to a research project on the study of religion among Dublin adolescents. The study could not have been undertaken without the generous co-operation of over two thousand and four hundred young Dubliners and their teachers. The expertise of past and present members of the staff of the Mater Dei Institute of Education, and of the Department of Education of the University of Manchester provided an invaluable resource from which to draw. The encouragement and financial assistance of the Episcopal Council for Research and Development and of my Community, the Daughters of Charity, made the research possible. To these people I am deeply grateful.

I am also indebted to those who encouraged the idea of using the research material as the basis of a book. In particular I want to thank Anne Kenna, Andrew McGrady and Hugh MacMahon, S.S.C., for their continued help and insightful criticism, Austin Flannery, O.P., and Patrick Wallace, P.P., for sharing their practical interest in and commitment to the growth in faith of young people, also Patricia Breathnach and Rose Curry who gave so much time and effort to typing the material.

*In memory of Rose and Brian MacMahon,
parents who communicated a living faith.*

Introduction

'In Christ you will discover the true greatness of your humanity.
He will make you understand your own dignity as human beings.'
These words were spoken by Pope John Paul to the youth of
Ireland in 1979. He reminded our young people that while they
'carry in their hearts the treasures which Irish history and culture
have given them they also share the problems that Ireland faces'.
When talking to the crowds at Knock, the pope pointed out: 'The
task of renewal in Christ is never finished. Every generation, with
its own mentality and characteristics, is like a new continent to be
won for Christ. The Church must constantly look for new ways
that will enable her to understand more profoundly and to carry
out with renewed vigour the mission received from her founder'.
How informed are we, the adult members of the Church, regarding the mentality and characteristics of this new generation of
Irish people? Is our knowledge objective and based on fact? Or is
it subjective and impressionistic? If we are not in touch with the
real needs, values and hopes of our young people, can we with any
confidence claim to 'look for new ways'? It can hardly be said that
the sense of urgency to which the pope referred characterises the
life and work of the Church in Ireland today. And yet we have
been asked to 'work for the Lord with a sense of urgency and with
the conviction that this generation, this decade of the 1980s ...
could be crucial and decisive for the future of the faith in Ireland'.
It has been said that 'no living community can exist without a
shared vision and a common cause. The kind of apathy and
alienation which can be detected in Ireland is a symptom pf the
absence of a sense of direction and hope'.[1] A number of challenges faces the Church in Ireland at this point in its history, but
many would agree that 'if there is one challenge above all others
which faces the Church in Ireland and in the developed world
generally, it is the challenge of showing that the living of the
Gospel is a service of freedom, justice and human dignity; that
these ideals are not a purely negative opposition to permissive
behaviour but an ideal worthy of the best and noblest and most
generous effort of which we are capable'.[2]

In order to help young people to mature in their faith and to come to the realisation that Christ is 'the way, the truth and the life' (Jn 14:6) we need a deeper understanding of what Christ, God and Christianity mean to them at present. We also need more detailed information on their perception and knowledge of basic Christian beliefs, how they celebrate these beliefs in personal and community worship, and how these beliefs influence day-to-day living. As we listen to young people and reflect on what they say, a degree of clarity will emerge which will enable us to discern strengths, needs and trends. A greater understanding of the actual experience and attitudes of young people will give us greater confidence to work with them, 'to find new ways'.

This need to listen to young people was strongy expressed by the Catholic Bishops of Ireland[3] in their letter to all concerned with the pastoral care of young people. A time of listening was seen as essential in order to appreciate the hungers, hurts, angers and hopes of young people as well as their attitudes in many areas and their experience of the Church in Ireland now.

The findings of the 1984 National Survey also point to the need for all who preach gospel values to the young to 'acquire the skills of reaching youth through the culture that is theirs, although this culture may be foreign to many adults'.[4] The acquisition and success of such skills is dependent on the accurate and sympathetic listening recommended by the bishops.

This book was written in the hope that it would be of use to parents, teachers, clergy and to all who work with youth – to all who seek to help our young people to grow in their knowledge and love of God. Knowing that youth minister to youth, it is also hoped that this book will have something to offer young people who wish to share their faith with others.

BACKGROUND AND OUTLINE OF THE STUDY

The findings of the 1973/74 National Survey[5] of Religious Practice and Beliefs in the Republic of Ireland showed that the age-group 21 to 25 had the lowest level of attendance at Mass, Confession and Communion. The same group had substantial numbers who were having difficulty with Church teaching. They did not find religion particularly important or relevant to life and did not rate it high in their scale of priorities. As might be expected, the 1984 comparison survey found that this group was more disaffected than in 1974.[6] 50% of the population of Ireland is under the age of twenty-five. The religious beliefs and practices of such a large group will have significant effects in the immediate and long term future of Catholicism in Ireland. Studies in England[7] have shown that, in the case of young English Catholics, dissatisfaction with the Church and religion in general can set in before the end of secondary school. Young people were rejecting the Church and religion before they had an opportunity to develop a mature understanding of it.

For those reasons it was seen as necessary to obtain information on the religious beliefs and practice of a younger age-group of Irish people. It was hoped that such material would identify areas of strength and weakness and provide a basis for planning and decision-making. Because published research was available on the religion of university students it was decided to work with a younger age-group – boys and girls in their final year of compulsory schooling. Since financial resources were not available for a national survey, the study was limited to adolescents living in County Dublin. The work was carried out as part of the requirements for the degree of Ph.D.

In the Spring of 1978 over two thousand fifteen-year olds completed a questionnaire dealing with religious beliefs and practice. They attended twenty schools which had been chosen at random from all of the schools in the city and county of Dublin. In each of the twenty schools three of these fifteen-year olds were also selected at random, and were asked to participate in an hour-long interview. 40% of the fifteen-year olds were boys and 60% were girls. Two years later five hundred and eleven seventeen-year olds completed the same questionnaire. Four hundred and fifty of them had answered the questions two years previously. 53% of the seventeen-year olds were boys and 43% were girls. The answers were statistically analysed, and the sex of the young person was taken into consideration.

However, when interpreting the percentage figures given in the book, it is important to keep in mind that the proportion of boys and girls in the group of fifteen-year olds is different from the proportion in the seventeen-year old group (fifteen-year olds: M=40, F=60; seventeen-year olds: M=53, F=47).

In preparing the questionnaire the help of young people, teachers, experts in religious education and theology was sought and the following areas of religion were selected:

Personal Religion

The fifteen- and seventeen-year olds were asked to describe in their own words what being a Christian meant for them. They were asked whether and if so how, belief in God would help them to become the sort of people they hoped to become, what beliefs were most important, what they found difficult about being a Catholic, what was the most important thing they had learned about their religion, what the Church did and should be doing for youth, whether it is possible to recite the Our Father and not work for social justice.

Knowledge and Strength of Basic Christian Beliefs

A number of questions was designed to enable the young people to disclose how much they understood about their beliefs. They were asked to explain in their own words to an enquiring non-Catholic what is meant by God, Jesus Christ, his life, death and resurrection, the Holy Spirit, the Trinity, the Church, the sacraments, Mass, the Great Commandment, the Blessed Virgin Mary, and what a Christian is meant to be.

Another series of questions was intended to help the young people to indicate the personal importance of basic beliefs. Examples of such beliefs are: 'God loves me'; 'I am responsible to God for the way I live'; 'Death is not the end'.

Worship and Religious Experience

An attempt was also made to find how often young people went to Mass, Holy Communion, Confession, how often they prayed, read the Bible, read a religious book or newspaper. In addition they were asked how often they felt the power and presence of God in the world about them, and in what circumstances such experiences occurred, e.g. at Mass, looking at the beauties of nature.

The Social Dimension of Religion

A large section of the questionnaire contained questions which were developed to obtain information on the extent to which religion influenced everyday living. These questions dealt with ultimate values, moral behaviour, religious principles, and the extent to which family, friends and Irish society were supportive of religion. They also dealt with the young person's perception of parents, priests, teachers of religion, goals of school, their own psychological well-being, social justice, missionary activity, Christianity and Catholicism.

The preceding areas – faith, knowledge, worship, experience and the social dimension of religion – were seen as central to religion. Studies on religion usually concentrate on one or more of them. By considering all of them, it was hoped that a religious profile of young Dublin Catholics might emerge. Fowler's[8] work on faith development, in which he proposed that faith develops as it progresses through a number of stages, also influenced the approach of this attempt to study the religion of Dublin adolescents.

THE STUDY AND THE PRESENT BOOK

The questionnaires were first administered in 1978, when the young people were fifteen. Two years later in 1980, when the young people were seventeen years old, a group of five hundred and eleven completed the questionnaire. As already explained four hundred and fifty of them had already answered the questionnaire when they were aged fifteen. A number of statistical techniques were used to analyse the responses of the fifteen- and seventeen-year olds. The study was completed in 1981 and was submitted as part of a Ph.D. thesis to the University of Manchester. A report was published in 1982 and presented to the Irish bishops who had subsidised the study. The present book is an attempt to present some of the more important findings in as non-technical and non-statistical manner as possible. Percentage figures are given to provide an indication of the strengths, needs and trends.

The study was carried out in 1978 and 1980. There is reason to believe that the situation today is less positive than it was then, that the factors which operated in 1978-1980 are still in force today. Reference is made in each chapter of the book to the findings of other studies involving young people and religion. Some of these studies were carried out more recently, and their results support the findings on which this book is based.

Each chapter also attempts to present an 'emerging message' directly related to the topic under consideration. In order to allow the young people to speak for themselves and to make their own contribution to the book the actual responses of a representative number of fifteen- and seventeen-year olds are included in each chapter. To maintain confidentiality the names used in the work do not refer to any identifiable person.

Urbanisation and affluence, the liberal-pluralist mentality and the increasing alienation from the Church of such groups as the unemployed, youth and women are among the factors which Bishop Donal Murray[9] discusses in his consideration of the future of the faith. For the young people who participated in the study these factors have always been part of reality. This reality is expressed by what they say about their beliefs and has shaped their very understanding of God, Christ and the Church.

Chapter One, 'Young Believers', examines the position of fifteen- and seventeen-year olds in relation to basic Christian beliefs. The importance of these beliefs and the young person's understanding of them is discussed and some significant patterns and trends are identified. What in fact do young people believe about God, Jesus Christ, the Holy Spirit? What changes take place between the ages of fifteen and seventeen?

Chapter Two, 'Young Worshippers', listens to what young people say about the Mass, prayer and the sacraments. It also considers the religious experience of young people. Difficulties and needs are reflected upon, and comparisons are made between the findings and those of other studies. Why do so many young people find the Mass boring? What is the difference between those who describe their view of the Mass in positive terms and those who have a more negative approach? When do young people experience the power and presence of God? How is prayer described? Are the sacraments seen as relevant to life?

Chapter Three, 'Young Church Members', attempts to assess what it means for young people to belong to the Church. Their perceptions of what the Church does for youth and could do are explored. Understanding of the nature of the Church and its missionary activity are also commented upon. Are young people attracted by the Church? Why are some alienated? What can be done for the positive young Church member? Are parents playing their part in helping their sons and daughters to develop confidence in the Church?

Chapter Four, 'The Young Christian and the World', tries to look at what it means for young people to be Christian in the world today. It considers the relationship between young people's aspirations for themselves and their belief in God. Difficulties in being a Catholic are identified and discussed. Consideration is also give to the social aspects of being a Catholic. How do young people see themselves coping with death and disaster? What might be their response to some everyday moral issues? What role do religious principles play in life? Do young people experience social support for being a Catholic? How do they understand the obligation to work for social justice?

Chapter Five, 'The Young Catholic and the Family', turns attention to the contribution which parents make to the religious development of their children. Young people's perceptions of their parents, the frequency and conviction with which parents talk about religion, and the influence of the parents' attitudes towards and practice of religion are analysed. The emotional climate of the home and the respective role of mother and father are considered. The relation between the home, school and the Church is also explored. Are parents the most influential people in their children's lives. How do young people judge the religiousness of parents? What are some of the characteristics of the homes of the young people who are most positive regarding religion?

Chapter Six, 'Towards a Preferential Option for Youth', focuses on the local community and the wider Church in relation to the pastoral care of youth. A number of questions are articulated and some tentative suggestions are made regarding future action.

ONE

Young Believers

Day-to-day living, worship, experience and knowledge are all part of being a Christian. While all these elements are inter-related, belief is at the core of Christian commitment. It is only within a set of beliefs about God and life that other aspects of Christianity have meaning. While there is an attempt in this chapter to look at the belief of young people, it is fully recognised that belief does not exist in isolation. Belief is celebrated in personal and community worship, experienced in many ways, expressed in a body of knowledge and lived out in daily life.

Since it is assumed that some knowledge of basic beliefs is necessary for their acceptance by adults and young people alike, belief and knowledge will be considered together. This chapter presents a profile of three young people who are seen as represen-ting particular groups – the young believing and practising Cath-olic, the confused and doubting adolescent, and the young alien-ated worker. The second section of the chapter looks at what young people 'know about what they believe' and the final section considers 'the emerging message' from the insights gained.

1. THREE YOUNG CATHOLICS

Seán: The Profile of a Young Believing and Practising Catholic
Seán was born in 1963 and lives with his family in North Dublin. His father works as a labourer for the County Council and his mother is a housewife. At the age of fifteen Seán hoped to become a trainee pilot, and at seventeen he had made up his mind to be a technician or a mechanic. His intermediate examination results and general attitude to study made it reasonable to assume that he would achieve a number of honour grades in his leaving certificate examination. During the last two years at school, Seán's understanding of religion developed, and his attitude be-came more positive.

When asked what it meant for him to be a Christian, he replied: 'Having complete trust in God and my fellow men, also being kind, friendly, co-operative and loving. It also means having a good relationship with others and fulfilling myself'. He described the person he hopes to be in terms of being a true Christian and leading a good and happy life, and he saw his belief in God helping him to realise this aspiration. While appreciating that he was 'not able to express myself completely' when speaking about religion he identified his belief in God, Jesus, the Holy Spirit, and the Blessed Virgin as among the most important religious beliefs in his life.

In considering the most outstanding things he has learned about his religion, Seán wrote: 'To do God's will is to love him. Because I believe in God I know I will be with him in everlasting happiness after death'. He saw the need for the Church to become more involved in youth activities and become more friendly with young people, in order 'to diminish any conflicting ideas'. Seán agrees with the statement from the Irish bishops' pastoral, *The Work of Justice*: 'I cannot truthfully and sincerely say the Our Father unless I work for a kingdom of justice, love and peace'. He adds: 'I can pray more confidently when I try to help others, especially the needy and when I am faithful and sincere with my family'.

Seán believes firmly in traditional Christian beliefs. When he was asked to consider a list of fourteen basic beliefs he described five of them as personally 'very important' and the remainder as personally 'important'. The following is the list of beliefs (they are not presented in the order given to Seán; the first five are those he regarded as 'very important'):

God loves me
All life comes from God
Jesus is alive because his Father raised him from the dead
I experience (meet, find) Jesus when I pray
Death is not the end
I am responsible to God for the way I live
Jesus shows us what God is like
Jesus shows us what people can be like
Jesus lived a life of love and service of others
The Holy Spirit helps me to live as one of God's family
The Church is the community of those who follow Christ in
    spite of the weakness of its members
As a Christian I am called to build a better world

I can be a good person in the future which lies before me, as I
am maturing every day
I can find love, truth and beauty in the world

Seán views priests as seeing all of the foregoing beliefs as 'very
important', other adults as seeing the majority as either 'very
important' or 'important' and most people of his own age as
seeing more than half of them as 'not very important'.

While Seán's understanding of these beliefs showed only a
moderate growth during the last two years at school his ability to
articulate them had developed. During the two year period Seán's
appreciation of the role of Christ in the life of a Christian became
more clear. At fifteen he had some understanding of the significance of having a personal relationship with Christ, and could say
that because of Jesus he could 'grow every day in his life and
kindness'. Two years later he felt that in some ways Jesus had
become the 'main animator of my life'.

If he was approached by a non-Catholic who asked for information about important beliefs of the Catholic community regarding
God and Jesus Christ, he said he would answer as follows:

God is divine, holy, loving, caring and sharing in our religion.
He is always there at your side, helping you in need, and
consoling you when saddened. Jesus is God the Son. He was
sent to this earth two thousand years ago to redeem man from
sin. He died on the cross for sin and redemption. His life
shows how a true Catholic should be good and faithful in all
things. Jesus is the example and prince of love and peace
between all men. His death and resurrection show his everlasting love for us. They also show us how to believe in God
and let us know if his will is done. We shall be resurrected to an
everlasting life with him.

Seán's explanations of the Holy Spirit, the Trinity, the sacraments, Mass and the Blessed Virgin Mary are rather similar. His
explanation of the Mass is of particular interest:

For me the Mass is the centre of my fulfilment in God. When I
go there I am spiritually enhanced and always find something
interesting and important to me in the Gospel and homily.

While this chapter is concerned mainly with belief and knowledge, it should be noted that Seán, at fifteen and seventeen, was
going to Mass and Communion every week. At seventeen he was
going to Confession several times a year. He described himself as

'very close' to his mother who is seen as 'very sure when speaking about religion'. In his experience religion lessons have been very helpful; his teachers of religion have been 'very good' and priests 'fairly good' in understanding the problems of young people.

Where belief is concerned, Seán can be seen as a representative of the young people who participated in the study. The majority of both fifteen- and seventeen-year olds indicated that they regarded most of the basic beliefs (which had been outlined for their consideration and are presented on p. 9) as personally 'very important' or 'important'. When the responses to the knowledge items (which dealt with the understanding of basic beliefs) are taken into consideration, Seán is seen as unrepresentative of the majority of the young people involved in the study. With two exceptions Seán's answers were categorised as 'good' or 'acceptable' while the greater proportion of the fifteen- and seventeen-year olds gave answers which were categorised as 'weak' and 'unacceptable'. Seán is not representative either of the small group who consistently gave 'good' or 'very good' answers to the same questions. When Seán's responses at fifteen are compared with those he gave at seventeen, there is evidence of a moderate increase in understanding. The responses of the majority of the young people who remained at school showed that they did not increase their knowledge or understanding of seven basic beliefs, that they had a loss of factual knowledge regarding three, and that they had acquired further knowledge and understanding of two. Finally, it may be said that Seán typifies the group of young people who at fifteen years of age have strong basic Christian beliefs, some ability to articulate them and an awareness that the Church can have a role in their lives, and who at seventeen are continuing to develop along these lines.

Áine: A Profile of the Confused and Doubting Adolescent
Áine was also born in 1963 and, like Seán, lives in North County Dublin. Her father is a butcher and her mother a housewife. At fifteen she had ambitions to become a journalist, but by the time she was preparing to sit her leaving certificate examination she had decided to apply for the army or gardaí. Her school record predicted success in examinations. At fifteen Áine was already questioning her attitude to religion, and was examining some of the basic teachings of Christianity. During her last two years at school she became confused, and shortly before leaving

wrote 'being a Christian means nothing to me because I understand nothing about it'.

On being asked to describe the person she hoped to be, Áine replied: 'When I am older and leave school I would hope to be a person that people could trust and talk to and I would like to make others happy'.

She did not see her belief in God helping her in this regard. In response to the question: 'What are important religious beliefs in your life?' Áine admitted at the age of seventeen that she had no strong religious beliefs, she just wanted to make others happy and be happy in return. She stated: 'I find being a Catholic difficult because I do not agree with what the Catholic Church says, and also I find it very hard to understand'. Her conclusion was that she had learned nothing important about religion.

When asked what the Church should do for youth, she felt that it should help young people to grow, but added: 'it should not ram all sorts of things down our throats, as I think it is doing now, always has been doing, and always will do'. Apart from indicating that it is personally 'important' that 'God loves me' she declared that the majority of the fourteen religious beliefs specified on the questionnaire were 'not at all important' to her.

When asked how she would explain important Catholic beliefs to a non-Catholic Áine replied that she would have to say that she does not know who or what God is, or who Jesus is. She would say that 'Jesus' life shows how man could live if he really wanted to, free from sin, pure and clean – although they'd probably go stark-staring mad at the end of it'. For her, Jesus' death and resurrection show that 'we must keep hoping. It shows us that after death there must be something, although I do not know whether to believe this or not because I don't understand it'. For her 'Mass is something we go to every Sunday'. In spite of her difficulties Áine is going to Mass every Sunday. While she is close to her father and 'somewhat close' to her mother, neither parent speaks to her about religion. Priests, in Áine's experience, have not been very successful in understanding young people's problems. Teachers of religion are described as having a moderate understanding of young people's problems, and religion classes are seen as 'not at all helpful'.

Áine, in her confusion about growing doubt, can be seen as typifying a growing number of young people. While the figures vary according to the question being asked, it can be argued that between 17% and 20% of both fifteen- and seventeen-year olds identify in many respects with Áine. While not outrightly reject-ing Christianity, they will need help if they are to continue to believe in God. Many of this group are engaged in a personal search for meaning and seem partially to find it in an individualis-tic relationship with a God who loves them. The community dimension of Christianity poses major problems for them. The adult members of the Church, on the whole, have failed to ex-press and celebrate the message of Christ in ways which recognise that young people are only in the process of developing intellec-tually, emotionally and spiritually. The role of the Church and the meaning of its message are not intelligible to a growing propor-tion of young Christians who are still receiving religious education and are in daily contact with adult members of the Church.

It is accepted that some doubt and confusion are inevitable experiences in the process of developing a mature faith. How-ever, it is also possible in today's world, which is not supportive of Christian beliefs and values, that, when the onset of doubt and confusion are not detected and catered for, they may quickly lead to unbelief. If the seeds of confusion and doubt are already apparent in a sizeable proportion of fifteen-year olds, it would seem essential to obtain more precise information regarding the relationship between age and the actual onset of doubt and con-fusion. Studies in England[1] have indicated that this may happen as early as the age of twelve.

Eoin: Profile of the Young Alienated Worker

Eoin, born at the end of 1962, is working as a stock room porter. He lives with his father, a painting contractor, and his mother, a housewife, in North Dublin. At the age of fifteen he, like Áine at the same age, was experiencing difficulty in accepting and understanding some of the basic beliefs and teachings of the Church. Being a Christian for him meant 'being ahead of the unknown and believing in a God which I feel is not really there'. He hoped to be honest, hard-working, trustworthy and kind, and did not see how God would help him to become that sort of person. The atmosphere around him was seen as the more power-ful influence. Fear of God was regarded by Eoin as the most important religious belief in his life. At fifteen he found it difficult to believe in religion, to love his enemies, and to keep the commandments. He also found actual belief in God and Christ difficult. The Church was seen as teaching young people to reject society and all human weaknesses while it should be seen as teaching them to understand the world of today.

Most of the basic Christian beliefs were seen by Eoin as 'not at all important' for himself. The information he would provide a non-Catholic about important Catholic beliefs was vague and indefinite. God was described as 'a being which man used to explain something which he did not know, but feared'. Jesus was seen as a 'being which man used to revive religion; his life showed he believed in peace, but did not know how to get it, and his death meant that he forgave us, so we could go to heaven'. At fifteen Eoin had ceased to pray, to go to Mass and the sacraments. He felt 'somewhat close' to both parents. His mother was described as being 'very sure' when speaking of religion and his father 'pretty sure'.

While teachers of religion were experienced as being fairly understanding of young people's problems, priests were seen as not understanding them well, and religion classes were regarded as not very helpful. Two years later Eoin felt he could not answer most of the questions put to him because he no longer practised. At seventeen, being a Christian meant believing in the truth and in himself, and he felt the Church should be helping young people to 'grow up good and honest'. He and his parents no longer spoke about religion. And in conclusion, he stated: 'I've never felt Jesus was anything in my life'.

Eoin in many respects represents the young non-practising worker who, leaving school at fifteen, to all intents and purposes has come to an end of all formal education in religion. The answers to a wide range of religious issues given by seventeen-year olds (who had left school at fifteen) were compared with the answers they gave two years previously. This showed that the most negative of the group of seventeen-year olds had also been negative at fifteen years. The comparison also revealed a considerable loss of factual knowledge among the early school leavers. Specific structures are needed at parochial level to enable them to integrate into the Christian community and to become adult Christians. Without such structures, and especially where family support is not available, regression is inevitable in the majority of cases.

2. WHAT THEY KNOW ABOUT WHAT THEY BELIEVE

Approximately two thousand six hundred fifteen- and seventeen-year olds were asked for information regarding eleven basic Christian beliefs. Their responses give some idea of what is uppermost in their minds concerning these beliefs. The eleven questions were introduced by the statement: 'Someome who is not a Catholic wants to know about important beliefs of the Catholic community. He has asked you for information. What would you tell him about each of the following?' Every response was examined to see if it could be described as 'very good', 'good', 'acceptable', 'weak' or 'unacceptable'. This was done in terms of what would reasonably be expected of young people who had been exposed to ten years of formal religious education to know about what they believe. With the assistance of teachers, experts in religious education, and theologians, a method was developed to enable the answers to be categorised as 'very good', 'good' etc. The answers of six young people (Rory, Maura, Dara, Fiona, Colm and Emer) are presented as representing the different types of responses regarding the following - God, Jesus Christ, the Holy Spirit, and on being a Christian.

'Very Good' Answers

Rory represents the young people who gave 'very good' answers to the request for information about basic beliefs. These answers, as already stated, were regarded as 'very good' in relation to what might be reasonably expected of fifteen-year olds. The standard was not raised for seventeen-year olds when it was seen that very few fifteen-year olds gave 'very good' answers. The fact that the same standards were applied to answers given at fifteen and then at seventeen made comparison easier, and facilitated the detection of any change which had occurred during the two year period. 'Very good' answers were usually seen to contain, however expressed, a sense of the main elements relevant to the belief under consideration. The number of fifteen-year olds giving 'very good' answers to eleven questions varied from 0.1% to 2%; and among the seventeen-year olds from 1% to 3% according to the question under consideration.

Rory – speaking about God, Jesus Christ, the Holy Spirit and on being a Christian:

> God is our creator, redeemer and friend. He and his work can be seen everywhere. He is omnipresent, loving and powerful.

God is the Father, Son and Holy Spirit. Jesus Christ is the Son of the Father and part of the Blessed Trinity. He became human and came to earth to save man. He was crucified, but rose from the dead, and ascended to heaven. He was to prove an example to us. The Holy Spirit is the love of the Father and the Son. Jesus left him to help us here on earth. He is the Spirit of love and unites us to God and to one another. A Christian is a baptised person who believes in God, who worships him and tries to live a good life in the way Jesus wants us to do.

'Good' Answers

Maura represents the group of fifteen- and seventeen-year olds who gave 'good answers'. These answers were less comprehensive than those categorised as 'very good'. The number of fifteen-year olds giving this type of response to eleven questions varied from 4% to 27% and from 1% to 35% of the seventeen-year olds according to the question being considered.

Maura – speaking about God, Jesus Christ, the Holy Spirit and on being a Christian:

God is the maker of all things. He is very powerful and lives with his Son, Jesus, and the Holy Spirit in heaven. God loves us and helps us. Jesus Christ is the Son of God. He died for our sins on a cross and was put there by man. Even as he died he shared his love for us on earth when he said 'Father forgive them for they know not what they do'. The Holy Spirit is God and guides us on the right path for heaven. He is always there helping us to know God better. A Christian is someone who believes that Jesus was sent by the Father to save us and who came in human form. He believes in the events of Jesus' life and lives by a moral code set by God.

'Acceptable' Answers

Dara represents the young people who tended to make general statements. The content was correct but limited. The number of fifteen-year olds giving these answers to eleven questions varied from 5% to 48% and from 5% to 38% of the seventeen-year olds, according to the question being examined.

Dara – speaking about God, Jesus Christ, the Holy Spirit, and on being a Christian:

·God is our Father in heaven. He made the earth and all its inhabitants. We pray to him for mercy and help. Jesus is the Son of God. He came into the world and was crucified for his beliefs and teaching. The Holy Spirit is God's spirit – a guiding spirit to give us courage and strength when we need it. A Christian is a follower of Christ.

'Weak' Answers

Fiona represents those fifteen- and seventeen-year olds who gave vague, very limited or very general answers. The number of fifteen-year olds giving this type of answer to eleven questions varied from 20% to 52% and from 3% to 62%of the seventeen-year olds according to the question under scrutiny.

Fiona – speaking about God, Jesus Christ, the Holy Spirit and on being a Christian:

> God is a person who looks after the world. Jesus is a man of love and kindness. The Holy Spirit gives us strength in Confirmation. A Christian is a person who loves his neighbour and God.

'Unacceptable' Answers

Colm and Emer represent the young people giving answers which were regarded as 'unacceptable'. Sarcastic and dismissive comments were seen in this way as were grossly inaccurate statements. Colm typified the first group, and Emer the second. The number of fifteen-year olds giving 'unacceptable' answers to the eleven questions varied from 4% to 31% and from 10% to 54% for the seventeen-year olds. The bulk of the 'unacceptable' answers given by the fifteen-year olds tended to be grossly inaccurate statements. At seventeen almost half the number of responses consisted of dismissive or sarcastic comments. The number varied according to the question.

Colm – speaking about God, Jesus Christ, the Holy Spirit and on being a Christian:

> God is a belief Christians have to reassure themselves that they have a leader and an immortal soul. I would only be able to say what the story is about Jesus – what it has been for so many years. To me there is no truth in it, but nevertheless, I would tell the story. The Holy Spirit is someone who guides us. But he does nothing for me. A Christian is a person whom priests think are supposed to set an example to the world by living without sinning.

Emer – 'God is one of the best men I have ever heard of. He does great things. Jesus is another man. The Holy Spirit is the third God of the Trinity. Everybody is a Christian'.

The following are among the general conclusions which can be drawn in relation to the requests for information regarding basic beliefs:

1. The greater proportion of the fifteen- and seventeen-year olds gave 'weak' or 'unacceptable' answers to the majority of the eleven questions.

2. Girls tended to give a higher level of response than the boys. However, at the age of seventeen there was a reduction in the number of questions to which girls gave the more acceptable responses.

3. The seventeen-year olds who were still at school gave 'better' answers than those who had left school at fifteen.

4. When the responses of the seventen year olds who were still at school were compared with the responses they gave two years previously, it was found that there was no change in the kind of response given to seven questions. The 'better' answer was given to two questions at the age of seventeen and to three questions at the age of fifteen.

5. When the responses of the seventeen-year olds who left school at fifteen were compared with those they gave two years previously the 'better' answer to eight of the eleven questions was given at the age of fifteen.

6. More than half of the fifteen-year olds gave 'very good', 'good' or 'acceptable' answers (the greater proportion falling into the 'acceptable' category) to the questions dealing with God, Jesus, Jesus' life, and on being a Christian. Less than half gave similar positive answers regarding Jesus' death and resurrection, the Holy Spirit, the Trinity, the Church, the sacraments, the Mass and the Great Commandment. Apart from the question on Jesus to which more than half of the seventeen-year olds gave 'very good', 'good' or 'acceptable' answers, the greater majority of the seventeen-years olds gave 'unaccpatable' or 'weak' answers to ten questions. The better answers of the fifteen-year olds may to some extent be attributed to the fact that 60% of the fifteen-year olds were girls, compared with 47% of the seventeen-year olds.

3. AN EMERGING MESSAGE

1. When asked to consider some basic Christian beliefs over 80% of the fifteen- and seventeen-year olds found it 'very important' or 'important' that God loved them, that they could find love,

truth and beauty in the world 'and that they could be good persons in the future which lay before them since they were maturing every day'. Apart from the belief concerning the Holy Spirit, the majority of the young people indicated a high degree of acceptance of traditional beliefs. Religious education has as one of its main aims the development of a believing community. The findings regarding the questions on belief in the study would seem to show that this aim is, at least to some extent, being realised.

2. However, the level of knowledge and understanding regarding these beliefs does not seem to have a sound conceptual basis. Lacking a reasoned foundation, belief tends to weaken in time. The personalisation of belief is a lifelong process. The finding that only a small proportion of the young people in the study had begun to see belief in Christ in relation to their own lives also raises questions about the solidity of the beliefs which seem to have a high degree of acceptance.

3. If it is agreed that one of the indications of the maturity of an individual's faith is the ability to give a positive and meaningful explanation of belief, it would appear that a considerable proportion of the young people in this study have not acquired this ability in relation to a number of important beliefs. The fact that seventeen-year olds were in their final year at school, or had left school, meant their formal religious education had come to an end without their acquiring this ability.

Studies of the nature of adolescent thinking and judgement have indicated that the content of an issue determines the level of thinking about it. Perhaps the cognitive content of some of the items investigated was of too abstract a nature for adolescents to understand adequately and to articulate. However, it must be pointed out that the standards applied in the examination of the answers of the fifteen-year olds were applied again two years later when the young people concerned were seventeen.

It is also possible to interpret these findings in the light of developments in religious education since the mid-1960s when the impact of the Second Vatican Council was being felt throughout the Catholic Church. Many teachers, feeling inadequate in the face of developments in catechetical and religious educational theory, allowed religious education classes to develop into discussion sessions. Prior to this time the majority of teachers who taught religion were not trained as religious educators. In many cases the emphasis in religion classes was on the mastery of the content of a limited number of basic text books. This approach to the teaching of religion made little demand on preparation by the teacher, or on the personal understanding of the material to be learned. When the change in emphasis due to developments in theology and religious education occurred in the mid-sixties, the majority of the teachers did not have immediate access to any alternative religious education programme. For this reason a planned and coordinated approach to the teaching of the Christian message was not always possible, and consequently, many young people did not acquire the necessary knowledge.

Recent developments in the religious education programmes for both primary and second level schools may result in the achievement of a more adequate level of knowledge among school leavers in the 1980s. But this is something which has not yet been established. It would seem important to continue to monitor young people's understanding of basic beliefs. Studies of adolescent English Catholics have led to the conclusions that many young adolescents[2] become disenchanted with the Church and cease to practise because of their childish misconceptions of God and religion. Similar studies with other denominations[3] show that religion is being rejected on a very low level of knowledge. As far back as 1965[4] it was pointed out that, where religion is concerned, growth in understanding only occurred where there was a degree of interest. It is difficult to know if the unsatisfactory level of knowledge found among a large proportion of the fifteen- and seventeen-year olds and the relative lack of development in knowledge and understanding during the last two years at school was due to lack of interest. As already pointed out, it could also be due to learning problems posed by the way important beliefs are expressed. Educators in other areas of the school curriculum are coming to grips with the learning problems connected with their subjects. While a similar effort by religious educators has already begun, further work needs to be done to promote greater understanding of basic beliefs. More suitable ways of communicating the Christian message in our time need to be found if lack of interest or learning difficulties are to be overcome.

Important as knowledge and understanding are, religious education cannot be limited to the acquisition of them. Turner (1979)[5] refers to the findings of other researchers that, when religious education is systematic and related to active Church membership, it would seem to foster a sense of purposeful progress. This raises a very pertinent question which will be considered in the final chapter – how can religious education programmes provide simultaneously for growth in the understanding of the basic message of Christianity and for active membership of the local Church community.

The Report on Irish Values and Attitudes[6] notes that in general the indicators show a clear and, in several cases, a strong shift towards vaguer beliefs, lower religious practice and more critical attitude towards the Church. This move towards vagueness was also identified in the study of the beliefs of County Cork teenagers.[7] A central finding of this study 'was the substantial degree of uncertainty among pupils with regard to the main beliefs of the Catholic faith'. The overall picture was seen as indicating a pervasive uncertainty which is more marked among boys than girls. While it was accepted that the problems of adolescents' crisis of faith is a familiar one, it was also seen that it calls urgently for an enlightened response. The fact that a quarter of the Irish people who believe in God are not too sure what sort of a God they believe in[8] suggests that the level of knowledge among adults may be contributing to the confusion of young people. The challenge posed by the confusion of young people and adults cannot be ignored. Growth in adult faith is dependent on the individual's commitment to ensure that stagnation will not take place. Concern for the Church of the future must not divert attention from the needs of the Church of the present. It has been long accepted that adult religious education is a priority in the Church. 'The Church has the problem of straightforward evangelisation, clearing up confusion about who God is, for example ... '[9]

The level of confusion and doubt which was experienced by a sizeable proportion of the fifteen year olds in the present study and the consolidation of this position at seventeen suggest that serious consideration should be given to studying the relationship between age and the onset of doubt and confusion. It is possible that in Ireland, as in other countries, young people may be taking a stance regarding religion before the age of fifteen and that this stance may be irreversible. The world today offers increasing support for non-belief. It would seem that serious attention needs to be given to the teenage 'agnostic'. To under-estimate the effect of confusion and doubt on adolescent faith is to put at risk the future of the Church in Ireland. It would seem that as never before young people need an opportunity to develop trusting relationships with adult members of the Church in which doubts can be voiced and support received. A number of the young people involved in the study spoke of the significant effect on their lives as Christians of meeting an understanding priest who helped them to distinguish between belief in Christ and confusion about some of the Church's teaching.

It has been said that the Church in Europe has lost the working class. It would seem that the Church in Ireland needs to show a sensitive and practical interest in the early school leaver if it is not to lose the young worker. The results of the study show clearly that in the years immediately following leaving school many of the young school-leavers cease to practise their religion and have difficulty in recalling what they learned at school.

The Church in Ireland has its Seáns, Rorys, and Mauras, as well as its Áines, Eoins, Daras, Fionas, Colms and Emers. The committed young Catholic as well as the confused and non-practising present a challenge. The former are signs of hope assuring us that much of what is being done is bearing fruit. It is important that we find ways to enable them to develop their potential as Christians and to minister to their peers.

TWO

Young Worshippers

This chapter begins with a cross section of reflections of young people on the Mass.

John and Sheila typify those of their peers whose knowledge and appreciation of the Mass grew during the fifteen- to seventeen-year old period, and who did not seem to experience any problem with the obligation to attend Sunday Mass.

John, at the age of fifteen, and attending Mass once a week:

> Being a Christian for me means thinking twice to see if what I am doing is what Jesus expects of me – trying to live the way Jesus wants me to live. It can be difficult to live Christ's way of life. At Mass all the congregation gather at a church and offer themselves to God, and then receive Holy Communion.

Two years later, still at school, and still attending Mass every week:

> Being a Christian means believing that Christ is alive today, and that I must try to be like him. It is believing in him, and trying to be like him. It is also participating in our local Church, praising and worshipping God. It is difficult to be like Christ when we are only human. At Mass a group of people, sharing the same beliefs, get together and pray to the one God. Mass is also a celebration where one can receive the Sacrament of Communion, which is really a unification with Christ through receiving his body. It is also a commemoration of Calvary.

Sheila, at fifteen and attending Mass every week:

> Being a Christian means I have something to believe in – that God created me and his Son saved me. It is not easy to live like Jesus. It is not easy to be always loving and forgiving. Mass is the gathering of God's people who worship him. At this gathering they receive Holy Communion, which symbolises the body and blood of Christ, who died for us.

Two years later, while still at school and attending Mass every week:

Being a Christian means having a goal in life – trying in my own way to follow Christ. Being a Catholic is not easy. It is not easy to live like Jesus, loving everybody as a brother or sister. It is so easy to lose your temper. It can be so difficult to forgive. The Mass is a community effort where everybody is involved. It is a reconstruction of the Last Supper and Good Friday and Easter Sunday.

Gerard, Patrick and Martin represent the significant group of young people who see their identity as Christians mainly in terms of going to Mass. In spite of their difficulties with the Sunday obligation they attend each week. But one wonders how much longer they will continue to do so.

Gerard, at fifteen, going to Mass every week:

Being a Christian means that I follow Christ and go to Mass on Sunday. Mass is the ceremony in which God is thanked and praised by the people. I don't find being a Catholic difficult, except I find Mass boring at times.

Two years later, still at school and attending Mass every week:

Being a Christian means going to Mass every Sunday. I see Mass as the celebration of Christian belief. Probably the greatest difficulty I experience in being a Catholic is understanding and taking for granted all the unanswered questions.

Patrick, at fifteen, attending Mass every Sunday:

Being a Christian means I go to Mass every Sunday. It means I also try to forgive people and live by the commandments. I don't find much difficulty about being a Catholic, apart from going to Mass. The Mass is where people go to pray to God.

Two years later, still at school and attending Mass every week:

Being a Christian means going to Mass on Sundays, living by the commandments, and helping round the house. It is difficult having to go to Mass. When you go to Mass you listen to the word of God in the Gospel.

Martin, at fifteen and attending Mass every week:

Being a Christian means trying to get on with my brothers and sisters and anyone I might get in contact with in my situation, also going to Mass. Everyone must go to Mass; it is the basis of our religion. Even among my classmates it is difficult to say that we must go to Mass. Those who don't go really play me down and sound as though they are right. The Mass is the way to receive Holy Communion regularly.

Two years later, still at school and attending weekly Mass:

> Being a Christian means upholding certain morals, which the Church, school, and my parents have tried to teach me. Lately, at this stage, it is difficult to be taught anything. Therefore, we should be left to make our own judgement and not told what to do. At present, I find it difficult to be told to go to Mass every Sunday. I wish I could be left make my own choice. The Mass is the means by which we profess our faith, by which we show we are believers. I think praying alone or in small groups is better.

Fiona, Mary and Kevin resemble those whose attendance at Mass began to decrease during the two year period. They seem able to justify their growing non-attendance.

Fiona, at fifteen, attending Mass every Sunday:

> Being a Christian means I should love God more and act as a good Christian. I have been given the privilege of being called to be a Christian. At Mass the priest offers God on behalf of all of us. I find it difficult to go to Mass, and find it boring when I get there.

Two years later, still at school and attending Mass several times a year:

> Being a Christian means I must be the person I am and not having to change just to please God. I find it hard to practise religion and to live by the Bible. The Mass bores me. It is just a speech about Christ.

Mary, at fifteen and going to weekly Mass:

> Mass is the worship of God by a congregation, adoring, praising and thanking him.

Two years later, working as a receptionist and going to Mass two or three times a month:

> I go to Mass to widen my knowledge of God and of life. I don't believe in formal prayer and think you are closer to God when you are talking to him.

Kevin, at fifteen, attending Mass every Sunday:

> To be a Christian I must be kind and honest. I am at the stage where I am not sure I should be going to Mass every Sunday. It is so boring. The Mass is re-uniting in God – saying you are sorry for all your sins.

Two years later, working as a hairdreser, and attending Mass several times a year:

At this stage I am not sure whether or not I am a Christian. I don't believe in going to Mass, I think I don't believe in God. Basically, being a Christian means being helpful and honest. It is very hard to listen to the so called Mass today. Half the time they don't even talk about religion at Mass.

Susan, Siobhán and Joe exemplify the group of young people whose attendance at Sunday Mass had begun to lessen before the age of fifteen. Many of these adolescents seemed to have a very limited idea of what is involved in being a Christian and to be in the process of rejecting religion.

Susan, at fifteen, going to Mass two or three times a month:

The Mass is something I go to sometimes. It is a drab place and is boring. The same things are said each Sunday. Going to Mass is the thing I feel most difficult about being a Catholic. For me, being a Christian means believing in the Father and talking to him regularly.

Two years later, still at school, and going to Mass several times a year:

The Mass is the boring thing which happens every Sunday in the church. God is there and is meant to be in each of us. It is hard on Catholics having to go to Mass every Sunday – I seldom go. The hardest thing is having to lie to my parents about going. Being a Christian means I try to be kind and loving.

Siobhán, at fifteen and rarely attending Mass:

I find it difficult to say what being a Christian means to me. I do know that the Mass has no meaning for me. I think the whole idea of confession is wrong. The whole Catholic religion has nothing for me, so I don't practise it. Going to Mass is just a drag.

Two years later, still at school and rarely attending Mass:

Being a Christian means I do what I feel to be right to live my life as best as I can, do what I can for others, trying to accept the faults of others, and putting up with hardships in the best humour possible. The Mass still has no meaning for me. The readings and gospels are in old English and are monotonous. Priests and nuns are old-fashioned. Because the Mass – or the way it is celebrated – is out of date, people don't participate when bored.

Joe, at fifteen attending Mass two or three times a month:

Being a Christian means believing in God and the after life. At the moment I find nothing difficult about being a Catholic, apart from going to Mass and confession. You could say Mass is a ceremony in which we offer thanks to God in the Church and pray to him.

Two years later, still at school and no longer attending Mass:

By faith I am an atheist. But I could describe the Mass as a ritual performance in praise and worship. I no longer see myself as a Catholic, so I do not practise.

These responses illustrate a number of trends which emerged in the overall analysis of the responses of the fifteen- and seventeen-year olds to the questions dealing with the Mass. A very small proportion spoke of the Mass in terms of God's people celebrating together, remembering Christ's life, death and resurrection, and the sharing by Christ of his life with us. The young people who had a relatively mature understanding of the Mass did not appear to have a problem with weekly Mass attendance. When asked what they found difficult about being a Catholic, they did not refer to the Mass; instead they gave evidence of a struggle in personalising a lived faith. They had problems with the challenge to love and forgive. In their responses to the question, 'What does being a Christian mean to you?' they referred to the call to live as followers of Christ. It would seem that they did not see their Christian identity solely in terms of Mass-going.

Young people with a more limited understanding of the Mass appeared to experience Mass as one of the major difficulties in being a Catholic. They also tended to see their Christian identity in terms of going to Mass. For them on the whole Mass is an experience to be endured. Approximately one in four of the fifteen-year olds and one in three of the seventeen-year olds would fall into this category. A larger group of over 40% of both age groups focussed on ritual and gave little evidence of meaning. For them, Mass was the main difficulty in being a Catholic. The weekly obligation was resented and described as very boring, a drag, or a dreary dull hour. The majority of them no longer attended Mass every Sunday. A small number indicated that they rarely attended. Religion meant very little to them so the Mass was completey dismissed.

FREQUENCY OF MASS ATTENDANCE,
COMMUNION, PRAYER AND CONFESSION

78% of the fifteen-year olds and 65% of the seventeen-year olds attended Mass at least once a week. Girls had a higher level at attendance than boys. Had there been an equal proportion of boys and girls in both groups, the figures might have been slightly lower for fifteen-year olds, and slightly higher for the seventeen-year olds. 42% of the fifteen-year olds and 25% of the seventeen-year olds went to Holy Communion every week. One in four of both groups went at least once a month. Almost half of the fifteen- year olds and two out of every five of the seventeen-year olds prayed every day. Approximately 70% of both groups prayed at least once a week.

Almost half of the seventeen-year olds and three quarters of the fifteen-year olds went to confession several times a year. When interviewed about their understanding of sin, the fifteen-year olds' responses seemed to fall into three categories. Almost equal proportions saw sin as an offence against God (disobeying him and 'turning one's back' on him), or in terms of concrete actions involving breaking the commandments, or in relation to childish misdemeanours, such as 'stealing biscuits'. This last group seemed to consider the notion of sin as irrelevant to their present life style. Only a small number of the fifteen- and seventeen-year olds read the Bible, a religious book, or a religious newspaper.

The Sacraments

When the fifteen- and seventeen-year olds were asked to explain what the sacraments are to a non-Catholic friend, it was found that three in every ten of the fifteen-year olds and four in every ten of the seventeen-year olds could name the majority of the sacraments, and add an explanatory comment. The remainder were unable to recall more than five and to make more than non-specific statements.

The following are examples of what some young people had to say about the sacraments:

Rory (representing a 'very good answer' given by 1% of the fifteen-year olds, and 2% of the seventeen- year olds. These answers were categorised as 'very good' because they included, however formulated, a sense of the following points: (1) the sacraments as encounter with God; (2) the sacraments as reveal-

ing life's meaning; (3) the sacraments as bringing about change.
The sacraments were also correctly named).

> There are seven sacraments and they were left by Jesus to us
> here on earth, so we may know, love and serve God:
> 1. Baptism in which God comes to us and in which we are
> made children of God.
> 2. Confession, in which all sins, big and small, are forgiven
> and we are reconciled with God.
> 3. Communion, I think, is the most important sacrament, as
> we receive the Body of Christ.
> 4. Confirmation, in which we receive the Holy Spirit with
> his gifts.
> 5. Holy Orders, in which men are ordained priests to give
> the sacraments.
> 6. Marriage is a joining together of man and woman.
> 7. Sacrament of the Sick, to bring us God when we are sick
> and dying.

Maura: (representing a 'good answer' given by 4% of the
fifteen-year olds, and 8% of the seventeen-year olds. These
answers usually included two of the points specifies for a 'very
good' answer, or a less adequate expression of the three points, as
well as the correct naming of the sacraments).

> In my opinion their purpose is to help people's minds, hearts
> and souls come closer to God. They also help us to change and
> grow as Christians.

Dara: (representing an 'acceptable' answer given by 27% of the
fifteen-year olds, and 32% of the seventeen-year olds. These
answers usually included one of the points specified for a 'very
good' answer and contained the correct naming of the
sacraments).

> Seven celebrations of God's family.

Fiona: (representing a 'weak' answer given by 30% of the
fifteen-year olds and by 27% of the seventeen-year olds. A 'weak'
answer was one which included reference to fewer than five of the
sacraments with a non-specific statement).

> Baptism, Confirmation, Marriage, Communion, Confession.
> They are gifts.

Colm and Emer: (representing an 'unacceptable' answer given
by 39% of the fifteen-year olds and 31% of the seventeen-year

olds. Inaccurate or dismissive statements or reference to only two or three of the sacraments were categorised as 'unacceptable').

Colm: 'I think there are eight of them.'

Emer: 'Confession, Communion, Baptism.'

Prayer

Many of the young people who pray – and over 50% stated that they prayed several times a week – felt that prayer involved listening to God. The majority also felt that God listened to them. They were aware that they might not get what they prayed for. However, there was an increasing awareness as they got older that prayers for strength and for the gift of being able to love were always answered. A large number declared that they did not like set prayers. They preferred to just 'talk and listen'. When thinking about God a number of fifteen- and seventeen-year olds had a sense of being loved, of peace and security. A smaller number spoke of a sense of power and majesty. A similar proportion described their feelings about God as 'mixed'. There were times when they were angry and confused. They realised they did not understand 'why God does the things he does'.

Religious Experience

An effort was made to investigate the frequency with which the young people involved in the study felt the power and presence of God in the world around them. They were also asked to identify the people, events or things which initiated such experiences. 63% of both age groups indicated that they had such an experience at least once or twice in their lives. Over 40% often had the experience. The beauties of nature, being alone in a church, and the experiences of death were seen as the most frequent initiators of such experiences for the seventeen-year olds. The beauties of nature and being alone in a church were also connected with religious experiences by over a third of the fifteen-year olds.

Prayer meetings, retreat experiences and crisis moments were also mentioned as times when God's presence was experienced. At these times the young people concerned felt that God was very near them. When speaking about a charismatic prayer meeting Michael said: 'I felt that I was being taken over – God was filling me with his love'. Anne, while reflecting on a retreat, remarked, 'For the first time, I felt God was very real – that he loved me and would always be there'. Frances, in considering her experience of God's presence noted, 'Sometimes in the chapel, the sense of his presence is so strong, also when I am in bed praying. I never kneel down to pray. It almost frightens me that Christ is so near'. For John, 'last Christmas was the first time I really felt God was near me. I just know why I am here. Like Jesus I know I have a job in life!' In relation to times of trouble or sorrow, Denise commented, 'I know God is there, I turn to him when in trouble. He gives me strength and things usually work out. But when my uncle died I stopped going to Mass for a while. I had trusted God and he let me down. But I am back at Mass again. I just have to keep on trusting him'.

Only 30% of the fifteen-year olds and 21% of the seventeen-year olds admitted to experiencing 'the power and presence of God' at Mass. The fact that such a small proportion of adolescents do not associate Mass with a religious experience gives substance to the possibility that motivation for attendance comes from legalism or social pressure.

AN EMERGING MESSAGE

1. A small number of fifteen-year olds (6%) rarely or no longer attend weekly Mass. It would seem that the pattern of non-attendance began before the age of fifteen.

2. The majority of the fifteen-year olds who were positive in their attitude towards Mass had a good understanding of it and of other aspects of their faith. They were also positive at the age of seventeen.

3. When significant difficulties were experienced at the age of fifteen, Mass attendance had decreased by the age of seventeen. For the most part minor difficulties at fifteen were more pronounced by the age of seventeen.

4. A relatively large proportion of young people attend weekly Mass because of parental pressure. Guilt at non-attendance was related to the pain caused to parents.

5. A large number of young people see their identity as Christians/Catholics in terms of attendance at Mass. For many of them Mass constituted the major difficulty in being a Catholic.

6. Only a minority claim to experience the power and presence of God at Mass. Over 40% of both age groups saw little meaning in the Mass. For them it was a boring experience. When difficulties with the Mass were elaborated upon, it would seem that problems lie in the selection of readings, in homilies which have

little relevance to the life of young people and which seem to have little religious content – 'There is no good news or guidance in them' – and in an approach to celebration which does not allow for variety or participation. The large attendance at Mass was also seen as a problem. Preference was expressed for small group and folk Masses. Among young people there was a feeling of resentment regarding the fact that the importance of the Mass was stressed by the home, school and Church. It was often presented as the highlight of the week, while the actual celebration of Sunday Mass was seen as an anti-climax or an over-rated experience.

7. Personal prayer was valued by the majority of young people. They saw it as a means of expressing their relationship with God and the majority who were questioned in some detail about prayer spoke of it in terms of listening and talking to God. The power and presence of God was also experienced in the more solitary moments – while praying alone in a church, while reflecting on the beauties of nature and while trying to come to terms with illness, death and suffering.

8. The majority of both the fifteen- and seventeen-year olds had a limited knowledge of the sacraments and an inadequate understanding of their relationship to life.

These points would seem to raise some questions which are all too familiar: How can the actual onset of non-attendance at Mass be identified, its causes known and responded to? What can be done to make the Mass a more meaningful experience for young people? What practical steps can be taken to help parents, teachers and clergy to present the Mass as an integral part of the life of the Christian, as a way of expressing and celebrating a living relationship with God and the Christian community?

American studies[1] on the religious attitudes and behaviour of youth have shown that the considerable decline in frequency of attendance at religious services need not be construed as total alienation from that Church. While it was obvious that attendance at church and prayer were less important in the life of the adolescent than they were ten years ago, some young people were seen to remain firmly committed. Research sponsored by the English General Synod Board of Education[2] found that in most cases, as far as non-Catholic adolescents were concerned, church-going ceased around the age of twelve to fourteen, when it was experienced as boring. It was also seen that only a small number of those interviewed felt at home in a church and in no case could it be claimed that any of the young people identified either emotionally or aesthetically with any liturgical celebration. Investigations with groups of young English Catholics[3] showed that two fifths of fifteen-year olds attending Catholic schools in the Southwark diocese were not attending Mass at least once weekly. It was concluded that there was clear evidence that the process of lapsation from this 'institutional requirement' was well under way in the early years in secondary school.

Another English study[4] dealing with young people between the ages of sixteen and twenty revealed that 47% of the Roman Catholics complain that their usual Sunday worship is boring, compared with 31% of the Anglicans and 16% of the young people who attend one of the Free Churches. It was also noted that while Roman Catholic teenagers are more inclined to think of their Sunday worship as 'boring' they are not inclined to think it is irrelevant to their lives. They were, however, also the group most prone to feel that the Sunday worship of their Church is out of touch with young people. The findings of this particular study led to the conclusion that teenagers seem able to cope with boredom provided the overall service seems relevant to their lives. Those who had ceased to find Mass relevant had stopped attending.

The National Survey of 1973/74[5] showed that the age-group which had the lowest level of attendance at Mass (78% weekly as oppposed to 91% for the overall population) was the 21-25 age group. It was concluded that this finding could be seen as 'a life cycle phenonomen, a generational phenonomen, or an indicator of long term social changes, or indeed, a combination of two or all of these factors'. The more recent study of Cork teenagers' belief, practice and prayer life[6] showed that 81% attended Mass at least once a week. While 82% of the girls went to Mass on Sunday and another 9% went several times a week, only 68% of the boys went to Mass on Sundays, and almost 2% also attended several times a week. It was noticed 'that the higher the population density the lower the Mass attendance'. This finding and the lower attendance by boys would help to account for the figure of a 65% attendance at Sunday Mass by the seventeen-year old Dubliners of whom 60% were boys, and the majority of whom live in high density areas. The Cork survey also presents the picture of a large number of young people receiving Holy Communion while not believing in the Real Presence. This confusion may reflect the lack of clarity about who God is, which was noted in the Irish Report of the European Value Systems Study. this European study found that among Irish people there was a clear and, in several cases, strong shift towards vaguer beliefs, lower religious practice, and a more critical attitude to the Church. A large proportion of the fifteen- year old and seventeen-year old Dubliners (almost 50% of the fifteen- year olds and 62% of the seventeen-year olds) had a very vague knowledge of the Mass.

It is inevitable that lack of clarity concerning the nature of the Mass, a failure to experience God's presence at Mass and a seemingly deficient celebration of the liturgy would lead to lack of appreciation and non-attendance by young people.

The implications of persistent non-attendance at Mass were considered by Michael Paul Gallagher.[7] He notes that the process of 'distancing' oneself from God and religion seems to go through a number of stages of which the first is 'abandonment of regular attendance at Mass and the sacraments'. While not identifying non-practice with non-belief, he points out that the abandonment of practice can be a key step in the direction of a deeper confusion over faith and eventual loss. It is pointed out that when practice has played a dominant role as the expression of religious commitment, its abandonment leaves the greater void, and it has been estimated that four years of non-practice can be practical unbelief. Gallagher feels that two opposite errors must be avoided: 'either putting so much emphasis on practice that one reduces Christianity to ritual performance, or being so dismissive of the importance of community worship as to under-estimate its crucial role in supporting the faith of most people'. The fact that in Ireland today there is growing support for non-practice could mean that in a few years this support will become one for non-belonging. Because so many young people of both the age of fifteen and seventeen see their identity as Christians in terms of attendance at Mass, the implications of their non-attendance need to be taken seriously. Careful consideration also needs to be given to helping young people to develop a relatively comprehensive understanding of what it is to be a Christian and to enabling them to become personally committed to Christ.

THREE

The Young Church Member

There are a number of ways of looking at the Church, for example, the Church as institution, the Church as the community of the people of God, the Church as sign, the Church as servant. Since the Church as an institution poses problems for many young people, the primary focus of this chapter is on the Church as an institution.

The Church as an institution is a reality with which young Catholics have to come to terms. Their perception of it as an institution is on the whole limited to their experience of it as a member of a particular parish. In order to understand how young people see the Church, the fifteen- and seventeen-year olds involved in this study were asked two questions: What does the Church do for youth today? What should the Church do for youth today? Because attitudes towards the Church are also determined by knowledge and belief, they were asked to explain to a non-Catholic what the Church means to Catholics. In addition, they were asked to indicate the personal importance of the belief that 'the Church is the community of those who follow Christ in spite of the weakness of its members'. It was felt that answers to questions regarding the missionary role of the Church might throw further light on the extent to which young people value being members of the Church. The replies to these questions will also be considered in this chapter.

A very small proportion of both the fifteen-year olds (3.5%) and seventeen years olds (2.5%) saw the Church in very positive terms. It was seen as an agent of meaning and identity which contributed to personal growth and significance. The answer of one fifteen-year old is an example of the type of response:

> The youth of today are disoriented by the world. But the youth of the Church have something to aim for – God. The Church guides youth and gives a sense of direction.

A large proportion (15%) of the fifteen-year olds and 22% of the seventeen-year olds made a more general but a still positive statement, acknowledging the Church's contribution. The following typify these statements:

> The Church teaches youth, or tries to teach them, how to be good, to respect their elders and to love others.
>
> The Church helps youth by bringing across its message at youth level.
>
> The Church fosters in young people a love of God and an understanding of right and wrong.

A substantial number (31%) of fifteen-year olds and 28% of seventeen-year olds emphasised concrete services given by the Church without giving any evidence of appreciating the significance of the service. They spoke of the Church as:

> Organising trips to Knock and running youth clubs.
>
> Providing recreational facilities and organising summer projects.
>
> Bringing youth together.

Criticism was voiced by 19% of the fifteen-year olds and by 7% of the seventeen-year olds. They cared enough about the Church to offer criticism, but did not make any other comment. For them:

> The Church does nothing. The Church still lives back years ago. It does not see youth.
>
> The Church tends not to see youth – except to criticise.
>
> The Church does very little, it tends to see youth as a pack of vandals.

A considerable proportion (22%) of the fifteen-year olds, and 41% of the seventeen-year olds showed indifference to what the 'Church was doing for youth'. Their responses can be summed up by a single word, 'Nothing'.

WHAT SHOULD THE CHURCH DO FOR YOUTH TODAY?

The proportions giving very positive answers are again small. 2% of the fifteen-year olds and 5% of the seventeen-year olds felt that the Church should provide opportunities for youth to develop a mature identity within the Church based on the recognition of the potential of youth to enrich the Church. The following are among the suggestions put forward by this small but important section:

Get the youth involved so that they are more helpful in the Church. Then they will see their place in the Church.

Encourage the youth to plan an active role in Church affairs. But first the Church must listen to what the young say, and see what they do.

Help the youth to take care of the old, the deprived and lonely, to feel part of the parish.

A second group also gave constructive suggestions. While lacking the notion of service as expressed by the previous group, they recognised the importance of relationship between the Church and young people, and the need for mutual understanding. Almost one in four of the fifteen-year olds and one in three of the seventeen-year olds showed this awareness. They asked that:

The Church have youth clubs run by priests where youth would meet priests in a social setting, where they could get to know each other and be able to help with religion and other problems.

The Church have more contact with youth, see their problems and see the help that is needed.

Arrange meetings so that youth and clergy can meet, talk about God and difficulties met by youth.

Half of the fifteen-year olds and approximately a third of the seventeen-year olds made suggestions which emphasised an intellectual view of the Church:

Organise talks and discussions on religion.

Have conferences about Mass etc.

Explain the Bible and have better sermons.

A considerable proportion of both the fifteen-year olds (14%) and seventeen-year olds (25%) felt either that the Church couldn't do much more or dismissed the idea of the Church having anything to offer youth.

Girls tended to give more positive responses than boys. The seventeen-year olds who remained at school had more constructive perceptions of what the Church should do for youth than the seventeen-year olds who had left school two years previously.

A small number of both fifteen- and seventeen-year olds saw the Church as a community of God and community of service. For them 'the Church is the body of people who believe in God and in the fact that he sent his Son from heaven in human form to save us and to show us how to love each other'. Similar, though less developed, responses were given by 14% of the fifteen-year olds and 12% of the seventeen-year olds. Their responses could be summed up by the answer of a fifteen-year old:

> The Church is the body of people who believe in the Catholic faith. They pray together frequently. In the Church people are supposed to be brotherly and equal.

The Church was seen primarily as an institution by 16% of the fifteen-year olds and 23% of the seventeen-year olds. The institution was described in general terms 'as the body of Catholics under the pope', or more specially as 'the priests, pope, bishops, cardinals, and most important the people'. Approximately half of the fifteen- and seventeen-year olds explained Church in terms of a building for religious purposes. A small proportion dismissed it as 'crap' or gave inaccurate statements ('It is like a God because we worship there every Sunday'). Almost 60% of both fifteen- and seventeen-year olds indicated strong assent to the belief that the 'Church is the community of those who follow Christ in spite of the weakness of its members'.

THE CHURCH AND ITS MISSIONARY ACTIVITY

When people value something, they usually like to share it with others. The Christian is one who has been asked 'to go and tell all nations', to share the good news of Jesus Christ. It was felt that **the** answers to questions dealing with the Church's missionary **nature** and activity would throw further light on the attachment of young people to the Church. The fifteen- and seventeen-year olds were asked the following questions: 'What do missionaries do?' 'Every follower of Christ has the obligation to do his part in spreading the faith - What does this obligation mean for your life?' and 'How important is it for the Church to have missionaries today?'

The Personal Obligation to Spread the Faith

A quarter of the fifteen-year olds and almost an eighth of the seventeen-year olds see missionary activity as an essential dimension of day-to-day Christian living. They spoke of this personal obligation as involving:

Acting in a Christian way to spread the Christian message by actions.

Spreading the faith by my actions and by my words - acting in a Christian way.

Spreading the faith by love and kindness in my ways of acting and speaking of God when I can.

Almost 30% of both the fifteen- and seventeen-year olds limited the obligation to particular actions such as:

Talking about religion to friends who don't fully believe in God. My friend finds it hard to believe. I try to help him by encouraging my friends to go to Mass.

In going to the sacraments and Mass and letting people see I practise my religion.

A number of both the fifteen-year olds (9%) and seventeen-year olds (16%) were open to missionary endeavour, but did not see any possibilities of such action in their present situation. The following typify their responses:

This obligation does not mean much to me at the moment because for a person of my age there is not much of an opportunity to spread the faith.

I don't think I have the ability to spread the faith like Christ did, because I don't think people would listen to me, but I would be willing to try.

It does not mean much to me as I am young.

A large proportion (17%) of the fifteen-year olds and 37% of the seventeen-year olds were negative in tone declaring that they felt no obligation to do their part to spread the faith.

Young People's Perception of Missionaries

A very small proportion of the fifteen- and seventeen-year olds showed a relatively comprehensive knowledge of the role of the missionary. They referred to the four main aspects of the life of a missionary describing them in terms of men and women who: (1) gave their lives, (2) proclaimed the word of God to people who had not heard it, (3) are concerned with total development,

(4) appreciate the riches which these new people bring to the Church. Half of the fifteen-year olds and 35% of the seventeen-year olds described missionaries in the light of two of the foregoing points. The following are examples of their answers:

> They help first of all by trying to grow crops and modernise living conditions. In everything they mention how Jesus helps them and gradually the people get to know Jesus.

> They preach the word to people who have not heard it, at great risk sometimes to themselves.

> They go to foreign countries and bring Christ closer to people. They teach about this.

A considerable number gave more limited answers. For them the missionary tried to convert non-Christians or helped deprived people. Only a small minority were completely negative or dismissive.

The Importance for the Church to Have Missionaries Today

The biggest proportion of both fifteen- and seventeen-year olds recognised that some form of missionary activity was essential for Christianity or saw its effect in a deepening appreciation of our gift of faith. Their responses are exemplified in the following:

> It is very important for the Church to have missionaries, but we must remember it is not only missionaries who have the obligation to spread the faith. 'Go tell everyone' is for us all.

> It is important because it helps us to remember how well off we are and to remember to value our faith.

> It is important because without missionaries the Church would not grow, would not have new members.

A substantial number of both age groups, 17% of the fifteen-year olds and 37% of the seventeen-year olds, either rejected the idea of missionary activity or showed a complete lack of interest.

YOUTH'S PERCEPTION OF PRIESTS, TEACHERS OF RELIGION, RELIGION CLASSES AND SCHOOLS

Priests, teachers of religion, religion classes and schools are often associated with the institutional Church. Brief questions were put to the young people in the study concerning each of them. While the information is limited, it is worth noting. Only a small percentage of both fifteen-year olds (11%) and seventeen-year olds (9%) felt that priests did not understand the problems of young people. 20% of both age groups felt that they had a limited understanding, while over 60% indicated that priests had a very good or good understanding. The results are similar, though slightly more favourable, for teachers of religion. 47% of both age groups found religion class very helpful or fairly helpful. The remainder indicated that in their experience such classes were not very helpful, or not at all helpful. Schools were considered in relation to their goals. Over a third of the fifteen- and seventeen-year olds perceived their school as putting Christian values into practice, enabling pupils to recognise right from wrong, and teaching Christian doctrine. Almost a quarter felt that schools had the latter two as goals and less than a fifth of young people indicated that they felt that their school had only one of these goals – to teach Christian doctrine.

AN EMERGING MESSAGE

It would seem that seven clear points emerge from these young peoples' reflection on the Church:

1. One in five of the fifteen-year olds and two in five of the seventeen-year olds involved in the study felt that the Church is doing nothing for youth. They can be said to be disenchanted with the Church or alienated from it. The Church as far as they are concerned has done nothing for them.

2. Many of these disenchanted young people were more positive in considering what the Church should do for them. It could be said that, in spite of their disappointing or negative experience to date, they had a vision of how being part of the Church could contribute to their lives.

3. A significant minority of fifteen- and seventeen-year olds had written off the Church. Their experience of the institutional Church was so negative that they could not imagine it having anything positive to offer.

4. While a substantial number saw the Church's commitment to youth limited to the provision of youth clubs and recreational facilities, almost one in five of the fifteen-year olds and one in four of the seventeen-year olds saw the Church contributing to their search for personal meaning and growth. They requested that the Church listen to youth, find ways of enabling them to contribute to the parish community, provide opportunities for the clergy and young people to meet and develop a mutual understanding.

These young people want to develop as people within the Church and to arrive at a more mature understanding of their faith.

5. On the whole the fifteen- and seventeen-year olds were positive in their attitude to priests and teachers of religion. The more favourably disposed of the seventeen-year olds were still at school. The situation of the alienated young worker and the unemployed young person manifests itself again. Who is responsible for them or is even interested in their pastoral care?

6. A considerable number of both age groups had little knowledge of or commitment to the Church's missionary nature and activity. It can be argued that such understanding and commitment demand a level of maturity which is not characteristic of the majority of young people. However, the positive answers of many of the fifteen- and seventeen-year olds show that the negative answers cannot all be attributed to immaturity. It can be difficult for many young people to become committed to the growth of a Church which seems blind to their needs and aspirations in their own parish and country.

7. When the fifteen- and seventeen-year olds were asked to explain what Catholics mean by the Church, more than half described it in terms of a building. Research has shown that adolescents between the age of thirteen and fifteen have difficulty in forming a concept of community. It would seem that particular attention needs to be paid to the way the Church is taught as well as to the way it is experienced by its young members. The responsibility of helping young people to develop an understanding of the Church as a community from which one receives and to which one gives, belongs to the family and parish, as well as to the school. The task of the teacher is hampered when the only experience of the Church as a community is that of the Sunday Mass. The people who are given particular responsibility for the religious education of adolescents and for their pastoral care need to come together with parents and other committed adult Christians. Young people mature as Christians by being with other Christians, and by participating with them in the community and liturgical life of the parish.

The foregoing points raise a number of questions. Is the Church prepared in a practical way to meet the needs of the more positive of its young members by involving them in the life of the parish? Is it prepared to give time, thought and personnel to finding meaningful ways by which teenage parishioners can contribute to the local Church, identify with adult believers and find their identity as persons within the Church? Is it prepared to reach out to its young alienated members, the majority of whom are unemployed or early school leavers? Because of their stage of development and social conditions, these young people come across as bored, apathetic or aggressive. They pose a particular challenge to the Church.

A number of recent studies,[1] which investigated different aspects of the Church, throw further light on the position of young people within the Church. The inadequacy of the Church as a human institution is compounded when emphasis is put on attendance at a Eucharist which seems to ignore the needs of young people. An investigation into the involvement of English Catholic teenagers[2] in the Sunday Mass showed that one in three hundred of them had an opportunity to exercise leadership, compared with one in five in the Free Churches.

It is not surprising that another study with young English Catholics found little evidence of a sense of belonging to a Church experienced mainly as an inadequate institution.[3] In an unpublished study[4] of Irish teenagers' concept of Christ and of their relationship to him, it is found that for the majority of Catholic pupils the school ranked as the most important source of information about Christ; for some parents ranked first, and for a small number the Church was ranked first. The situation was reversed for Protestant pupils. The Church ranked highest as a source of information about Christ, with parents and schools both having an important role. The author points out that the question may be asked 'whether the school has taken over the responsibility of the Church and parents in the religious formation of the adolescent'. The question may also be asked, 'How committed schools and the Department of Education are to the religious formation of the adolescent'.

The role of parents as members of the Church in the religious development of their children is also referred to in the Irish Report of the European Value Systems Study. One of the authors, Michael Fogarty, points out: 'For parents, there is also the question of how far they are willing to take up again their share of responsibility for developing their children's religious faith and confidence in the Church'.[5] Among the clearest trends on relations between parents and children is the declining importance attached by parents to developing religious faith. He also emphasises the Church's problem in restoring its credibility, especially with younger and more educated people. The finding that half of the Irish people have less than 'a great deal' of confidence in their Church was seen as one of the major shifts in Irish Catholicism. The time has come for the Church to be seen and experienced in ways other than as an institution. This is not to deny the need for the institutional dimension of the Church, merely to put it in context. The responses of the young people in the present study to their experience of the Church would indicate that if the Church continues to fail them it will become increasingly irrelevant in Irish society. However, the greater proportion of both fifteen- and seventeen-year olds indicated a desire to belong to a Church which would allow them to contribute to its life and which would enable them to mature. They also gave some directions and suggestions concerning their involvement. But will the Church as a community of believing and caring adults (including parents, teachers and clergy) listen and respond?

FOUR

The Young Catholic in the World

The acid test of one's religion is its living out in the reality of daily life. It can be said that wherever Christians go they bring with them a personal attachment to Jesus Christ and a commitment to live as his followers, respecting their neighbour and working for peace and justice. This attachment and commitment varies from person to person. In this chapter an effort is made to examine young people's understanding of what it is to be a Christian, and to look at some of the ways this understanding is reflected in life. The first section of the chapter deals with what being a Christian means for young people, the relationship between what they hope to be and their belief in God, the difficulties they experience in being a Christian and the most important things they have learned about religion. The next section looks at some of the social aspects of being a Christian – coping with death and disaster, responding to moral issues, appreciating the significance of God at specific moments in life, the putting into practice of Christian principles and the obligation to work for justice.

'BEING A CHRISTIAN MEANS FOR ME'

'Being a Christian means for me ... '
The answers to this item show that the largest proportion of both the fifteen-year olds (47%) and the seventeen-year olds (59%) thought in terms of life style.

> My relationship with others is affected because of my belief in God.

> To be a good person and obey the ten commandments.

> That I always have someone to turn to when things go wrong – someone who cares for me.

A smaller number (23%) of the fifteen-year olds and 10% of the seventeen-year olds mention belief or faith as the essence of being a Christian. Their answers, as exemplified by the following, also indicate a personal relationship with Christ.

Believing in Christ and telling your children about God and helping them to believe.

Means I believe in God the Father, his Son Jesus Christ and the Holy Spirit.

That I have something to believe in – that God created me and the Son saved me.

Almost 11% of the fifteen-year olds and 7% of the seventeen-year olds made explicit reference to Christ and showed an understanding that Christianity is a way of life specified in the way Jesus lived, died and rose again.

Thinking twice to see if what I am doing is what Jesus expects of me – trying to live the way Jesus wants me to live.

Having a goal in life – by trying to follow in Christ's footsteps.

That Christ is alive today, and that I must try to be like him. It is believing in him and trying to be a better Christian. It is participating with our local Church in praising and worshipping God.

Answers which were regarded as weak were given by 8% of the fifteen-year olds and 14% of the seventeen-year olds. These answers showed a concentration on the observance of religious duties and laws when these are seen as a constraint from outside:

Going to Mass on Sundays and Holy Days because I have to.

Doing what the pope and bishops say.

Means I must carry out my duties like any other Catholic.

Negative answers or those having no positive religious implications were given by 3% of the fifteen-year olds and 10% of the seventeen-year olds. An example of such answers would be: 'Makes no difference'.

Girls at both the age of fifteen and seventeen gave more positive answers than boys. When the answers of seventeen-year olds were compared with those they gave two years previously it was seen that on the whole the 'better' answer was given at the age of fifteen. Major differences were not found between the answers given by seventeen year olds still at school and seventeen year olds who left school at the age of fifteen.

While the first item on the questionnaire asked the young people to consider what 'Being a Christian means for me ... ' the final item asked them to respond to 'In my life Jesus means ... ' The trend in the answers was in many respects similar for both questions. The greater proportion of the young people responded positively, speaking of Jesus Christ in terms of a personal relationship. It was also found that in general the 'better' answer was given when the young people were fifteen years of age. The results show that the greater proportion of the fifteen- and seventeen-year olds had positive perceptions of what it is to be a Christian and of the role of Jesus in their lives. Only a small percentage had a deeper Christocentric religious commitment. Jesus Christ was seen as an attractive person, answering many of the ideals of the young person. But this attractiveness developed into commitment only for a relatively small number. It can be argued that progression from 'being attracted by' to 'being committed to' requires time. However, the results show that for many young people deterioration rather than growth occurred during the fifteen to seventeen period.

'The Type of Person I Hope to Be and my Belief in God'
When they were asked to consider the type of person they hoped to be, the majority of fifteen- (62%) and seventeen-year olds (58%) concentrated on one area of development – the personal or social – without including a spiritual orientation. A small number spoke in terms of personal and social development also referring to the religious dimension of life. The proportion giving rather vague or purely self-centred statements varied from 16% for the fifteen-year olds to 30% of the seventeen-year olds. The following are examples of such answers:

A relaxed person with a decent job.

A good job.

A leader of some kind so that people will look up to me.

The responses to the question 'Do you see your belief in God helping you to become that person? If so, why?' are quite revealing. The greater proportion of seventeen-year olds (39%) indicated an awareness, however clumsily expressed, of man's inability to do good on his own. However, 19% of them had a purely self centred approach and 26% gave responses which were regarded as 'unacceptable' because they gave evidence of a completely external morality. ('It is socially acceptable to believe'). Other responses contained a vote of 'No confidence' in God ('No – you make your way alone'), or consisted of cynical statement ('you must be joking'). The pattern for the fifteen-year olds was more positive. 40% of them showed a consciiousness of man's basic orientation towards God. A substantial proportion (24%) indicated an awareness of man's inability to do good on his own. But 17% gave 'unacceptable' responses.

It is generally agreed that during the period between fourteen and eighteen years of age the young person is building, integrating and consolidating an image of himself and that stability regarding this image is not reached by the majority until the twenties or early thirties. The fact that the fifteen-year olds are in the early stages of this process of image building, and the seventeen year olds are in the midst of the more difficult phase may account for the less positive answers of the latter. However, it is interesting to note that, when considering what the Church should be doing for young people today, a number of the fifteen- and seventeen-year olds felt that it should help them in their quest for identity.

'The Most Important Thing I Learned about Religion ... '

The greater proporation of both fifteen- (75%) and seventeen-year olds (57%) gave answers to this question showing a general awareness of God's continuing involvement with mankind. Within this group a smaller number would have shown an understanding that they, like Christ, would die and rise again, and that they had a personal relationship with God who loved and forgave them. 6% of the fifteen- and 16% of the seventeen-year olds limited their answers to general statements like: 'it is the one true religion'; 'being a Catholic'; 'it is the chosen religion – chosen by God to speak the truth'. Negative and superficial answers were given by 6% of the fifteen-year olds and 25% of the seventeen-year olds. Girls at both fifteen and seventeen gave 'better' answers than boys, and seventeen-year olds who were still at school gave 'better' answers than those who had left two years previously. However, a comparison of the responses of those still at school at seventeen with the responses they had given two years previously showed that in general the 'better' response was given at the age of fifteen.

'What I Find Difficult in Being a Catholic ... '

When considering what they found difficult about being a Catholic, 3% of the fifteen-year olds and 4% of the seventeen-year olds gave evidence of a struggle in personalising faith. They spoke about:

Living a life like Jesus did, loving everybody as a brother or sister, when it is so easy to lose your temper or be selfish.

Difficulty in living Christ's way of acting – doing what he did.

Trying to live a good life and trying not to do wrong – really loving God and my neighbour. Trying to be like Christ when we are only human.

Answers showing reflection, personal searching and an awareness of central mysteries were given by 14% of the fifteen-year olds and 11% of the seventeen-year olds. These responses reveal an emerging quest for meaning and the following are examples of them:

Trying to believe God is good when tragedies happen.

Accepting biblical stories when there is no proof.

Believing God had no beginning or end.

The highest proportion of fifteen-year olds (47%) and seventeen-year olds (34%) gave general statements which lacked any questioning of central beliefs. They tended to speak about:

Having to do good and love everybody.

Concentrating on the Mass, giving up things for Lent.

Keeping the commandments.

Dissatisfaction with the Church (when the Church is seen only as an institution of rules and regulations) was expressed in a variety of ways by 8% of the fifteen-year olds and by 17% of the seventeen-year olds. They saw difficulties in terms of:

Too many rules.

All the rules and regulations involved – and which are irrelevant

The formality and dullness of religion – which should be brought up to date.

19% of the fifteen-year olds and 35% of the seventeen-year olds gave answers which indicated a lack of reflection or naivete, e.g. 'nothing at all'.

THE YOUNG CHRISTIAN IN LIFE SITUATIONS

Coping with crisis situations, making moral decisions, experiencing the joys, successes and sorrows of life, putting religious principles into practice and facing issues of justice, are all part of the daily life of the Christian. Responses to them reflect inner convictions. In order to obtain some indication of the social dimension of religion, young people were asked to consider a variety of topics. In examining their answers it is appreciated that verbal statements alone are available. No claim is made regarding what fifteen- and seventeen-year olds would actually do in given situations. However, their ideas on the various topics give an indication as to how they might act and show whether or not they are aware of a Christian way of responding.

Coping with Crisis Situations

The fifteen- and seventeen-year olds were presented with four crisis situations, typical of those occurring in real life, and which call for some kind of response, which in turn, reflect an approach to reality. These four crisis situations were developed by Greeley, McCready and McCourt (1976).[1] There were six possible responses to the situation, and those were seen as reflecting hopefulness, religious optimism, secular optimism and pessimism. Greeley, McCready and McCourt describe religious optimists as achieving belief in an optimistic future, by denying present evil, and secular optimists as denying evil in the world but not depending on God to support their denial. Pessimists are presented as either hostile or resigned to the tragedies which befall mankind – they make no appeal to God, and do not express any connfidence in a positive outcome. The hopeful are seen as those who show some understanding of the existence of evil while at the same time holding to their belief that the situation will end in a way that is ultimately positive and influenced by what Greeley and McCready call 'a benevolent reality'.

The crisis situations dealt with the news that one has a year to live, the destruction of life and property by a storm, the approaching death of a parent, and the birth of a handicapped child. The percentage of fifteen-year olds giving hopeful responses varied from 28% to 11% according to the item. With the exception of the item dealing with fatal illness, over 50% of the fifteen-year olds fall into the hopeful or optimistic categories. The percentage of seventeen-year olds giving 'hopeful' responses varied from 15% to 29% – and again with the exception of the first item, dealing with fatal illness, the majority of the repsonses fell into the 'hopeful' or 'optimistic' categories. The fact that the first item was directly addressed to the adolescent, presenting him or her with the situation of his own death, may account for the high proportion of responses falling into the 'pessimist' category. Greeley, McCready and McCourt (1976) concluded in relation to their own finding that Catholic schools had a positive effect on producing a hopeful world view in people who had spent more than ten years in a Catholic school. This may account for the more positive responses of the seventeen-year olds who had spent over ten years in a Catholic school, while the fifteen-year olds would have been in their tenth year in such schools. While the changes which take place during the fifteen- to seventeen-year period are in the direction of hopefulness, the results show that quite a proportion of the adolescents had not integrated their Christian vision into a hopeful view of reality. In fact, almost as many as 30% in some instances of both fifteen- and seventeen-year olds would respond pessimistically in crisis situations. They would not appeal to God and would not express any confidence in a positive outcome.

Making Moral Decisions

Five multiple choice items dealt with familiar problem situations and consisted of two parts – action and moral reasoning. The situations were concerned with coming home to find one's mother 'very tired', 'the absence of the boss from work', 'an appeal to help a deserving cause', 'overhearing a plan to injure a player on the opposing team', 'the reaction to a mean action of another'. The greater majority of both fifteen- and seventeen-year olds saw themselves as responding positively to the situations. A considerable proportion also gave as a reason for their action 'primarily because I am a Christian' or 'in conscience I believe it is the right thing to do'. The findings also indicate that the change which took place over the two-year period was one which led to a higher level of moral reasoning. The highest number of responses, in which the young person said they would do nothing, were found regarding the item dealing with the appeal to support a deserving cause and the item presenting the mean action of a group of people. The reasons given for these responses reflected a lack of concern due to the frequency of appeals and the need to avoid trouble when unjust incidents involving others were taking place.

It could be argued that self-centredness and fear of group pressures account for 25% to 30% of both the fifteen- and seventeen-year old respondents giving these answers. While it is appreciated that the responses were verbal ones, and that the words and behaviour do not always correspond, it can be said that the responses to the five items indicate that the greater proportion of the young people were aware how they should act.

The Importance of God at Specific Times in Life

Six multiple-choice items were used to investigate young people's experience of the importance of God at specific times in life – in times of happiness, success, planning for the future, suffering, loneliness and death. There were four possible responses: 'very important', 'important', 'not very important', and 'not at all important'. More that 80% of both the fifteen- and seventeen-year olds indicated that to them God was either 'very important' or 'important' in the sad events of life – in times of suffering, loneliness and death. Over 60% of the fifteen-year olds and 70% of the seventeen-year olds felt that God was either 'very important' or 'important' in times of happiness, planning and success. When the answers of the seventeen-year olds who left school at fifteen were compared with those who remained at school, more of the former were found to see God as 'very important' or 'important' in times of happiness, success and planning. The results show that the greater majority of the young people have experienced the relevance of God in a variety of human experiences. They also suggest that during the last two years at school the process begins which leads to God being perceived as less important than formerly.

Religious Principles

The items concerned with religious principles were used by Nic Ghiolla Phádraig in the National Survey (1974)[2] and by Inglis with university students in 1976.[3] They were designed to obtain some information on the extent to which people felt that religious principles guided their free time activities, work life and life within the family. There were four possible answers: 'always', 'most of the time', 'some of the time', and 'never'. In the study with adolescents school life was substituted for work life. The answers of the fifteen-year olds showed that the greater proportion of them felt that religious principles guided them 'some of the time'. 17% indicated that religious principles never guided their behaviour at work or at school. The figure was higher (25%) regarding spare time activity. Similar trends can be observed in the results for the seventeen-year olds with the bulk of the answers indicating 'some of the time'. The figures for 'always' and 'most of the time' varied between 34% for the family and 21% for school/work, and spare time activities. The fact that the most positive picture is found regarding the extent to which religious principles influence family life would suggest that religion is seen as more relevant in the personal and private sphere of life, than in the more public areas of school/work and spare time activities.

When the results were compared with those obtained by Nic Ghiolla Phádraig and Inglis, it can be seen that a higher proportion of the fifteen- and seventeen-year olds answer in the 'never' category. It may be argued that this finding suggests that the younger people had a less developed understanding of religious principles and that they had not yet acquired the level of commitment or maturity necessary for living out Christian values. Perhaps it could also be said that the home is providing the necessary support for living Christian principles. The extent of peer group influence on school and spare time activities has still to be established. In other areas of the study it was found that young people saw their peers as less positive towards religion than themselves and adults in general. This leads to a consideration of the social support young people receive regarding their religion.

Social Support for Being a Catholic

It was decided to obtain some information on the extent to which young people felt that it was important for their friends, parents, Irish people in general and themselves to be Catholic. There were four possible answers to each question: 'very important', 'important', 'not very important', and 'not at all important'. Apart from the item 'importance for your friends' over 70% of the fifteen- and seventeen-year olds felt that being a Catholic was 'very important' or 'important' for themselves, their parents and Irish people in general. Over 50% said that it was 'important' or 'very important' for their friends. It would seem from the results that parents and Irish people in general are providing social support regarding religion for seven out of every ten of the adolescents involved in the study. Older people give the impression, presumably by what they say and do, that being a Catholic has personal value for them. However, young people form a large proportion in Irish society. The fact that 40% of both the fifteen- and seventeen-year olds concluded from what their friends said and did that it was 'not very important' or 'not at all important' for them that they were Catholics may have serious implications for the Church in the future. The support of others is necessary for the development of the individual's religion. Without the support of their friends' belief and practice, it is likely that when the young people in the study become parents, their religion will be considerably weaker than at present. A social climate and environment will then have come into existence which will support decreasing belief and practice among the next generation of children and young people.

Social Justice

The items concerning the understanding of social justice asked the fifteen- and seventeen-year olds to consider the following: 'I cannot truthfully and sincerely say the Our Father unless I work for a kingdom of justice, love and peace on earth. Do you agree with this statement? If so, why?' and 'How in Dublin today can a Catholic boy or girl really live out this obligation?' In their answers to the first of these questions, 5% of the fifteen-year olds and 17% of the seventeen-year olds showed a recognition that prayer and action are complementary in working for the kingdom. The following give some idea of their responses:

> Because the Our Father is all about justice and peace.
>
> If we listen to the words of the Our Father, they are telling us about peace, love and justice. So, if we mean them, we must work for what they say – we must work and pray.
>
> You say 'your will be done on earth as it is in heaven', and that can't come about if we don't work for a kingdom of love, justice and peace. Prayer and work go together.

Among 19% of the fifteen-year olds and 17% of the seventeen-year olds there was an emphasis on sincerity – meaning what you say and expressing prayer in action. They tended to make statements such as:

> We can truthfully say the Our Father if we mean the words.
>
> We can't all do work for justice – we can all pray.
>
> If you are earning your living all day, the best you can do is to pray at night – prayer can do a lot.

7% of both fifteen- and seventeen-year olds indicated a surrender to the inevitability of evil, with comments such as:

> There will always be fighting on earth, but you will have a clear conscience if you pray.
>
> There is little I can do about justice and peace.

We are just human and there is not much we can do.

Answers dismissing the obligation to work for justice were given by 28% of the fifteen-year olds and 47% of the seventeen-year olds. The following is an example of these answers: 'It is a load of rubbish – I cannot get peace on earth'.

When asked, 'How in Dublin can a Catholic boy or girl live out this obligation?', 16% of the fifteen-year olds and 14% of the seventeen-year olds showed in their answers a sense of responsibility anchored in their life situation which is reflected in the following:

Doing something positive like helping the old and needy.

Doing something spiritual like living your day in God.

By helping the old people in the parish and by being kind and friendly to everyone.

A smaller number had positive attitudes of service, but these were limited to a minority or to the future or to spare time activities, and were expressed in statements such as

Become a priest or a nun.

Be a lay missionary when I grow up.

Being prepared to do something when I am an adult.

48% of the fifteen-year olds and 40% of the seventeen-year olds emphasised giving and doing, but did so in vague, general or undemanding terms:

Being considerate.

Being nice to people and giving good example.

Praying to God for help.

A minority of both age groups referred to the pressures of society and an inability to do anything. 28% of the fifteen-year olds either could not answer the questions or made statements betraying lack of concern and commitment. 32% of the seventeen-year olds also indicated indifference.

The Irish bishops's pastoral letter *The Work of Justice*[4] states 'We are never allowed to make a separation between religion and life, or between the service of God and service of the neighbour. Neither can we ever separate charity from justice'. The findings of this study suggest that only a small proportion of the young people showed a moderate to good understanding of the Christian obligation to work for justice. A considerable number betrayed lack of concern or indifference. It would seem that at the end of the final two years at school there was a greater awareness of how to respond to the obligation, but there was not a corresponding development in the actual understanding of the obligation. The commitment to work for justice, it could be argued, is the outcome of a mature Christian faith. It would be unrealistic, therefore, to expect a more positive response from young people of fifteen and seventeen. It can also be argued that Christian faith can only mature if it is expressed in some form of Christian action. The indifference of some of the young people raises questions regarding the quality of the religious education which they received in the home, parish and school. If love of the neighbour is seen as an essential element in being a Christian, the indifference of a considerable proportion of the fifteen- and seventeen-year olds must be a cause for concern.

AN EMERGING MESSAGE

While it must be remembered that the religion of the majority of these young people has still to be reflected upon and personalised, many of their views make one wonder what will happen to them as they face the challenges of an ever more secular Irish society. Most of them are still untested by life and have lived in an environment which would claim and attempt to nurture Christian values. An examination of their answers to questions dealing with basic Christian issues reveals a number of points which merit serious consideration:

1. As these young Christians cope with the reality of daily living the majority would seem to be positive in their attitudes. They tended to see the role of Jesus in their lives in terms of a personal relationship, and being a Christian in terms of life style. They felt that God would help them to achieve their personal aspirations and would say, in one way or another, that the most important thing they had learned about religion was 'God's continuing and active presence in the world'. They also had a general appreciation of the difficulty of living out their religion. At no other time in their lives will they be so full of ideals, good will and energy. But is there an awareness at parish level that this is a time of decision-making for the majority of young people and that they need a leadership which is mature in its strength and sensitivity? What can parishes do at a practical level to enable their young members

to come in contact with adult members of the Church who are committed to Christ and to living the Christian way of life? In order to become committed and active Christians young people need to be in touch with adults who are themselves committed and active. It can be safely surmised that, without particular encouragement and guidance, a considerable proportion of these positive young people will find the challenge of living their Christian values in the consumer society of today too difficult or too idealistic. It would be unrealistic in today's world to expect overwhelmed or disillusioned young Christians to become committed adults.

2. A small proportion of these fifteen and seventeen-year olds had a more enlightened and committed approach than the majority of their peers. These are the potential active members of the Church. What is the Church at parish level doing for these very promising young people? Among them are the potential Christian leaders, but also among them are the potentially disillusioned.

3. There was a small but significant percentage who were negative in their views. They indicated apathy regarding Christian values and behaviour. Is the Church, again at parish level, prepared to reach out to them in a practical and enlightened way before they succumb entirely to the values of a consumer society? Without some specific pastoral care they are likely to become the most exploitable members of the consumer society. All young people, of course, need help to live their Christianity in a consumer and secular society, seeing the challenges and the difficulties. However, the least committed are most at risk.

4. While there was evidence to suggest that the moral reasoning of these young people had developed during the fifteen- to seventeen-year old period, a third of the fifteen-year olds and half of the seventeen-year olds had little understanding of the Christian obligation to work for justice. They expressed a surrender to the inevitability of evil or an inability to do anything because of the pressures of society, or they indicated indifference. Religious principles were found to operate most strongly in the family and to a lesser extent in the public sphere. The personal dimension to the religion of the fifteen- and seventeen-year olds, while still largely unreflected upon, seems to be in a more healthy position than the social dimension. Thought needs to be given to developing practical ways which will faciliate the integration of the per-

sonal and social dimensions of the religion of young people. Without a social context, a religion which has personal signifi-cance only becomes self-centered, serving mainly the needs of the individual. It ceases to be Christian.

5. Although the majority of young people felt that their parents and Irish people in general regarded being a Catholic as 'very important' or 'important', a considerable number felt it was 'not very important' or 'not at all important' for their friends. The peer-group of young Irish people constitutes a large proportion of the population. The impact of any perception of that peer-group should not be under-estimated. Consideration needs to be given to developing more ways of peer-group ministry. The ministry of 'like to like' needs to be studied and faciliated, particularly in relation to young people.

In the conclusions reached in the survey[5] of the attitudes of senior students in Co. Cork schools, towards religion, morality and education, it was remarked that many young people reflected the attitudes prevalent in society (e.g. in regard to travelling people, homosexuals, ex-criminals). Since these attitudes have manifested themselves in acts of social injustice and violence, it was felt that the findings pointed to the need for more focused consideration on principles of social justice as part of religious and moral education, and as part of preparation for life in a pluralist society. The need was seen as more pronounced in relation to boys' schools. In an attempt to answer the question, 'Are religious people prejudiced?', Anne Breslin[6] distinguishes between 'religious people' who are unquestioning and orthodox and for whom religion is a matter of private devotion and com-placent certainty and 'religious people' who are morally mature, socially responsible persons who endeavour to practise the Chris-tian virtues of compassion and justice. She concludes that it is among the former that intolerance is likely to emerge. Our schools attempt to produce the latter, but are they, in conjunction with the family and society, producing more of the former? An examination of the attitude of teenage church-goers in England to the society in which they live[7] showed that twice as many young people (45%) felt that it was within their power to do something about the problems which confront the world today, as compared with those who felt they can do nothing (23%). The remaining 32% cent were regarded as being unconvinced they could do anything or overwhelmed by powerlessness. The majority of these young teenagers were seen as showing a real concern about Third World and more local problems. These rather positive findings bring to mind a comparison of surveys of Catholics in England and Wales, with those in Ireland.[8] While Mass going was much higher in Ireland, active involvement in the Church, as measured by membership of parish organisations, was much higher in England and Wales than in Ireland. If the majority of adult Irish Catholics do not have a conscious social committment, it is not surprising that young Irish Catholics have difficulty in understanding the Christian obligation to work for social justice.

An examination of the goals of American parents and religious educators regarding the religious education of adolescents showed that where Catholics were concerned there were eight important goals.[9] When these were ranked according to importance, the goal concerning social justice came second last. The finding is particularly interesting in the light of the fact that the first goal was moral maturity. An analysis of these results indicated that some of the goals, and among them the goal of moral maturity, were related more to total human development than to specific faith or Church commitment. In a discussion of three distinct elements of faith Avery Dulles (1977) claims that one of them – a vision of a just and compassionate world – should be a particular priority for Christians of today on account of the greater insight into the inequality of rich and poor countries and the inescapable deprivation and hunger of the world's poor. The low rating given to social justice in this investigation among parents and teachers was seen to indicate a genuinely low priority for it in religious education and youth ministry. It was also noted that the most strongly worded items on social justice received the lower rating. The more moderate the wording the higher the rating. This was seen as suggesting that parents and teachers preferred inter-personal ethics and general consciousness-raising to concentration on social justice issues and specific social witness. It was also noted that all denominations gave social justice a rather low priority and yet, as Bishop Cathal Daly[10] points out, 'the credibility of the Church will increasingly depend in future on her relevance to the problems of poverty and on the clarity and courage of her proclamation of social justice and her effectiveness in working for a more just society'.

An investigation of the religious effectiveness of some Australian Catholic high schools for boys[11] has indicated that pupils 'are more open to social justice concerns when they see religious staff giving a credible witness to a radical Gospel life-style dedicated to ideals of peace and justice and where the staff community as a whole is seeking to develop just working conditions for both lay and religious'. Explicit promotion of Christian goals and the practice of justice were seen as essential for the formation of a Christian community in the school setting. In his attempt to answer the question, 'Will our children have faith?', John Westerhoff[12] considers the role of the Christian community in relation to the parish. He describes how one Christian community saw their educational role. For them Christian education is all 'the deliberate, systematic and sustained effort made in any aspect of their parish life which enabled them as persons and as a community of faith to become more Christian in their individual and corporate lives'.[13] They felt that their Church's educational ministry could be judged by how well it (a) sustains and transmits the Christian faith tradition, (b) nurtures the expansion of faith and the spiritual lives of people, and (c) equips and motivates the Church and its members to fulfil their Christian vocation in the world. In order to realise this last aim Westerhoff saw the need

> (a) to be introduced to a community of faith engaged in mission and be provided with foundations for an awareness of corporate selfhood, justice, freedom, community and peace,
> (b) to be given opportunities to commit one's life to social causes for the reformation of Church and society,
> (c) to be equipped and motivated to engage in the reformation of the Church and society on behalf of justice, liberation, whole community, peace, and the self development of all people.[14]

In the discussion of a survey among seventeen- to nineteen-year old school leavers in Dublin concerning their concept of Christ and their relationship to him[15] emphasis was put on the need to present Christ as Lord to young people. It was felt that Christ should be taught so that he is 'allowed to harness unbounded energy, vital youthful zest and dynamism'.[16]

Young people who respond in action (CND marches, Peace Corps, or community service volunteers) were also seen as responding to Christ when he is presented as appealing to their idealism and speaking to their goodness and strength. It was regarded as imperative to affirm the lordship of Christ – 'the lordship of Christ present in the world, working out his purpose when he calls pupils and students to his service as technicians, industrialists, teachers, doctors, politicians, and common people'.[17]

To summarise, it would seem that a number of studies indicate that

1. More attention needs to be given to education in social justice and for life in a consumer and secular society.

2. The adult Christian community should become aware of the fundamental obligation to work to justice and the transformation of society.

3. It is possible for a Christian community to find ways of living the Christian vocation more fully and practically.

4. Young people need to develop a relationship with Christ who is Lord as well as friend and personal redeemer.

5. In order to educate for justice a school community needs explicitly to promote Christian goals and justice while at the same time seeking an integration of secular learning with the Christian tradition.

FIVE

Young Catholics
and their Families

While some young people are very much aware of their peers and others are anxious to meet the expectations of the peer-group, the majority acknowledge that their parents are the most influential people in their lives. Any consideration of young people's religion must take into account the role of the family and parents. In this study a cross-section of sixty fifteen year olds was interviewed in some depth concerning the significant relationships in their lives. They were chosen at random, and were left free whether or not to participate. The purpose of the interview was explained and nobody asked to be excused from participation. The remainder of the fifteen- and seventeen-year olds involved in the study were asked to give written answers to questions dealing with closeness to parents, closeness of parents, personal qualities of parents, and parent's confidence in speaking about religion. It was again stressed that people were free not to answer these questions. The numbers of those who chose not to respond varied between 8% and 15% This chapter will begin with extracts from some of the interviews, and then will deal with the answers to the written questions.

EXTRACTS FROM INTERVIEWS

The form of the interview was based on that used by Fowler[1] to study faith development in children, adolescents and adults. It dealt with four areas of the young person's life: (1) life review (outlining the main events in the life of the adolescent); (2) life-shaping experiences and relationships (the most influential people and events in the young person's life); (3) present values and commitments; (4) religion. The following questions are concerned with parental relationships and with some aspects of religion. It is hoped that the sequence of answers accurately reflects what was said and that it gives some insight into the significance of parental attitudes and behaviour for the religious development of adolescents. It should also be appreciated that a written account captures only a limited amount of the content and spirit of an inverview.

Cian

Cian is a fifteen-year old boy attending a boarding school on the outskirts of Dublin city. He has a good relationship with his parents, and the family seem to have a positive approach to religion.

Interviewer: What gives meaning to your life, Cian?

Cian: Enjoying myself and looking forward to life afterwards. Also keeping the commandments. I suppose I want to enjoy this life and be happy in the next.

Interviewer: Who are the most important people in your life?

Cian: My parents, brother, sister, relations.

Interviewer: How did you see your father when you were a child?

Cian: Caring, trying to do his best for all of us, I suppose.

Interviewer: How do you see him today?

Cian: The same way.

Interviewer: Has he any interests apart from his work?

Cian: Oh yes, golf and tennis.

Interviewer: Would you say he was a religious person?

Cian: Yes – religion is important for him. Every Sunday the routine in the family is to go off to the 11.3O Mass and he makes sure we go, no two ways about it.

Interviewer: Anything else that would make you say he is religious?

Cian: I remember going in to say good night one time, and seeing him kneel to say his prayers. He also has a feeling for 'down and outs', and gives to good causes. Loving your neighbour means something to him.

Interviewer: What about your mother?

Cian: The same, religion is important to her.

Interviewer: How did you see her when you were small?

Cian: The same as my father - caring for us all, and I see her the same way now.

Interviewer: What does religion mean to you?

Cian: It is important – you see it gives meaning to my life. I feel God listens to me. He wants me to treat people generously. Some day I will die and then I will be with God. My grandfather died a

short while ago, and that made me think. There is a purpose to life
– otherwise we would not be living.

Interviewer: What do you want to do when you leave school?

Cian: Work in the business at home. I like working in the shop,
and my Dad would like to have me there.

Dónal

Dónal is fifteen and attends a Dublin boarding school. He has a
good relationship with his parents, who have a positive approach
to religion and discuss it with him. His father's attitude has
obviously influenced him.

Interviewer: What gives meaning to your life, Dónal?

Dónal: Being happy and doing stuff that is important to me and
to other people as well.

Interviewer: Who are the most important people in your life?

Dónal: Parents and friends.

Interviewer: Has your father any interests apart from his work?

Dónal: Fishing and gardening.

Interviewer: Would you say he is a religious person?

Dónal: Yes, I would. I think he has it all worked out. He talks
to us. He knows there is a God and he believes in an after-life. He
believes we must do our best in this life to prepare for the next life.
But there are some things he does not agree with in the Church.

Interviewer: Would you say religion influences his life?

Dónal: Yes, you could say it does. He worships God and he has
a good conscience. He was offered a very good job in Saudi
Arabia and other places. But if he went it would mean there was
no one sufficiently skilled to do his work in Ireland. And that
would be the end of that particular work.

Interviewer: When you were small, how did you see your
father?

*Dónal: Quite differently from now _ he was the big man who
could do everything.*

Interviewer: And now?

Dónal: Seeing him more realistically – he has some faults and
there are things he cannot do. But I like him a lot.

Interviewer: How did you see your mother when you were a
child?

Dónal: A person who was always there to take care of me – to
pick me up when I fell.In. And what about today?

Dónal: In much the same way – she keeps the family together, and really does her best for everyone.

Interviewer: Would you see her as a religious person?

Dónal: Well in a way – no – but then I am not sure. She is a Protestant – and does not attend any services. But she thinks about it a lot.

Interviewer: What does religion mean to you?

Dónal: Well – like my Dad and my big brother – I know I am not here just to be here. We are here to do something with our lives. Some people in my year do not think about God or about life. They don't seem to think deeply. My religion has given me an optimistic view of life. It is a big factor in my life. I have a relationship with God and I pray.

Interviewer: What can you say about prayer?

Dónal: Well, I think when I am praying how much God did for me. After all, he did not have to create us. He did not have to share his love with us or send his Son back. That is love at its greatest.

Fidelma

Fidelma is a fifteen-year old attending a large post-primary school in north Dublin. She comes from a happy home in which religion is lived and discussed.

Interviewer: What gives meaning to your life, Fidelma?

Fidelma: God – you see he has a plan for us; my family and school are part of that plan. My family also gives me meaning.

Interviewer: Who are the most important people in your life?

Fidelma: Parents.

Interviewer: When you were small how did you see your Dad?

Fidelma: Every Friday we used to go to see him on our way to do the shopping. We brought him a present. He was big and loving. He was not out of reach. He was someone I could talk to.

Interviewer: How do you see him today?

Fidelma: Loving, and easy to talk to.

Interviewer: Has he any interests apart from his work?

Fidelma: Gardening, I garden with him. Sometimes I go to the races with him.

Interviewer: Would you say he is a religious person?

Fidelma: Yes, I would, although as a family we pray on our own. We go to Mass together and Confession. As a family we celebrated First Communion and Confirmation.

Inteviewer: Would you say religion came into his life?

Fidelma: Oh yes – he taught us at home, and he taught us to pray. And he works for the Vincent de Paul.

Interviewer: When you were a little girl how did you see your mother?

Fidelma: Someone who was always there, someone to turn to, and to talk to.

Interviewer: And what about today?

Fidelma: Someone who is still there – has the time for me and I can ask her anything.

Interviewer: Has she any other interests apart from nursing?

Fidelma: No – nursing and visiting.

Interviewer: Is she a religious person?

Fidelma: Yes, very religious.

Interviewer: Why do you say that?

Fidelma: Because any questions I have about religion, I always ask her and discuss them. Even though I may not be saying what is right, she always sees my point of view and listens.

Interviewer: How important is religion for you?

Fidelma: I would say, very important.

Liam

Liam is a fifteen year old attending a large new post primary school. He seems closer to his mother than to his father. Liam appears to judge the importance of religion in the home in terms of going to Mass.

Interviewer: Liam, what gives meaning to your life?

Liam: I suppose getting a good job – my mother and father are trying to get me one.

Interviewer: Who are the most important people in your life?

Liam: My family.

Interviewer: When you were a child how did you see your father?

Liam: He used to work out and come home with presents for us. It's different now because there are seven of us, and he is tired. He has a sore back, so I just don't want to ask him anything. I seem to be able to make up my own mind. Sometimes I ask him. He is alright.

Interviewer: Has he any interests apart from his work?

Liam: He has a sore back, but he likes fishing.

Interviewer: Would you say he is a religious person?

Liam: I don't know. The way he goes on it is important to him, but he does not go to Mass, not much. So I don't know really. I don't know what religion means to him.

Interviewer: When you were small how did you see your mother?

Liam: I used to ask her everything – I saw more of her. We all go to her for everything.

Interviewer: How do you see her now?

Liam: She relies on me with all the little ones. She needs me to give her a hand.

Interviewer: Has she any interests outside the home?

Liam: No – she has no time, not with all of us.

Interviewer: Would you say religion is important to her?

Liam: Oh yes – she was talking to me last night.

Interviewer: She talks to you about religion?

Liam: Yes – she said that she is going to make us go to Mass, and that she is not going to let us leave Mass until we are gone from her.

Interviewer: She goes herself?

Liam: Holy days and some Sundays. But some Sundays she has to stay with the little ones – they are too small to go.

Interviewer: How important is religion to you?

Liam: Not very important – it's how you carry out your daily life that matters. I see being a good Christian the way I am in the family.

Interviewer: What does religion mean to you?

Liam: Nothing apart from living a good life, and not doing anything bad not hurting anyone.

Angela

Angela is fifteen and attends a fee-paying secondary school. Her parents are estranged.

Interviewer: What gives meaning to your life, Angela?

Angela: Getting a good job, I suppose. I want to get a degree first, a good one. Then I can choose a career.

Interviewer: Who are the most important people in your life?

Angela: Well, I should say my parents, shouldn't I? But really my friends are now.

Interviewer: How did you see your father when you were a child?

Angela: He always gave me things, nice things, big things – but he did not read me stories or take me out like other fathers.

Interviewer: How do you see him now?

Angela: Much the same – kind, but too busy to talk to me. His work means a lot to him.

Interviewer: Would you say he is a religious person?

Angela: No, I would not; he does not seem to have any interest whatsoever. I feel he is an atheist, or an agnostic. One or the other.

Interviewer: What about your mother? How did you see her when you were a little girl?

Angela: Well she was good to me. She was always there.

Interviewer: And now?

Angela: We have grown apart. It is mostly my fault. My home is not a happy one, so I take it out on her.

Interviewer: Would you see your mother as a religious person?

Angela: No, not now. I think she was when I was small – but now she does not practise. Neither do I for that matter. She isn't interested in religion. Her main interest is the house and golf. But, to be honest, she does care about me. It is hard on her that Dad has no time for her – or me either.

Interviewer: What does religion mean to you?

Angela: Not much really, to be honest. I know it does mean something to the nuns, and to many of the other girls. But not to me.

Interviewer: Why do you say that?

Angela: I did not see much of it at home – did I?

Dominic

Dominic is a fifteen-year old attending a north Dublin school. While the family seem important to Dominic, he would appear to feel that religion did not have much significance for either parent.

Interviewer: Dominic, what gives meaning to your life?

Dominic: Wanting to be a carpenter.

Interviewer: Who are the most important people in your life?

Dominic: The family.

Interviewer: When you were a little boy how did you see your father?

Dominic: Seeing him come in from work, meeting him at the gate and getting my wages off him.

Interviewer: How do you see him today?

Dominic: Slowing down and getting older.

Interviewer: Has he other interests apart from his work?

Dominic: Carpentry and painting.

Interviewer: Would you say he is a religious person?

Dominic: No – he tells us to go to Mass, but he does not go himself, except at Christmas and funerals. But he is a good man all the same.

Interviewer: How did you see your mother when you were small?

Dominic: Being in the flat, cleaning and that, always there.

Interviewer: And now?

Dominic: The same, still caring for us.

Interviewer: Would you say she is a religious person?

Dominic: Well, she talks about religion, but she does not go to Mass.

Interviewer: And what about you – is religion important to you?

Dominic: Well God is, but I don't go. You can live a good life without religion, you know.

An analysis of the interviews confirmed the crucial role of the parents in the religious development of their sons and daughters. Practically all of the sixty young people interviewed accepted and valued their parents' point of view, to the extent that they were willing to permit this view to direct their own behaviour. That parents would pray and attend Mass was seen as significant in determining what appears to be a religious life. Mothers were acknowledged as good, involved in prayer, patient, faithful and Mass goers. In the greater proportion of cases fathers were seen as merely going to Mass. While some fathers did not attend Mass themselves, they insisted that their children should do so.

When parents were committed to their attitudes and behaviour and had a good relationship with their son or daughter, the young person was basically positive in his or her approach to religion. It would seem that the good relationship was a crucial factor. The most positive picture emerged in the situation in which parents talked about religion, gave evidence of having thought their position through, were committed to living their religion, and had a loving relationship with their children. The convictions and expressed views of fathers played a particularly significant role in the development of the convictions and commitments of sons. While the influence of a religiously committed and loving mother cannot be over-estimated, the expressed commitment of fathers seems to be directly related to strength of conviction in the young person. This was more obvious in relation to boys.

As small children, the majority of the young people interviewed saw their father as 'the greatest', 'able to do anything', 'the bossman'. To quote one fifteen year old, 'he was the Taoiseach in the house'. Fathers were also seen as 'caring and good'. The main emphasis, however, was on their strength and power. Mothers, on the other hand, were seen as primarily caring and loving, and that perception merely deepened with the years. While the fathers were no longer seen as all-powerful, with the passing years sons and daughters, on the whole, saw their fathers as 'human with faults and failings'; they were 'easier to talk to', 'more of an equal', 'loving and caring'.

While there was an obvious if implicit emotional attachment to fathers, it was not as clearly evident as in the case of mothers. The strength of the emotional attachment to mothers in almost all cases grew as children became older. 'I loved her then, but I love and value her even more now' seemed to be the attitude. Many of the fifteen-year olds also referred to their mother 'as being always there' and spoke of 'feeling close to her'. The fact that the greater proportion of the mothers concerned did not work outside the home would seem to indicate that the 'being always there' had the dimension of physical presence.

The responses to the questions in the interview also suggest that it was the more well-to-do and educated fathers who played an active role in the lives of the children. Sons and daughters of these fathers had a greater awareness of how they thought about religion and life in general. These fathers were also more frequently described as loving and caring. Their sons and daughters felt close to them and had some insight into what was important to their fathers.

ANSWERS TO WRITTEN QUESTIONS

Closeness to Parents and Closeness of Parents

62% of the fifteen- and seventeen-year olds saw themselves as very close to their mothers, with only 2% of the fifteen-year olds and 4% of the seventeen-year olds describing themselves as 'not at all close'. The remainder indicated that they were 'somewhat close'. The figures for closeness to fathers was lower. 48% of the fifteen-year olds and 45% of the seventeen-year olds considered themselves to be 'very close', with 6% of the former and 10% of the latter declaring themselves to be 'not at all close'. The remaining number regarded themselves as 'somewhat close'. Approximately 70% of both groups saw their parents as very close to each other.

Qualities of Parents

The young people involved in the study were asked to consider the following list of words in relation to their parents, and to select three which would come closest to describing them: 'competitive', 'warm and loving', 'dissatisfied', 'good at making decisions and firm', 'sensitive to others' needs', 'reserved (slow to show feelings and give opinions)', 'ambitious for himself/herself', 'satisfied'.

The majority of mothers were seen as 'warm and loving', 'sensitive to others' needs'. Fewer of the fathers were regarded as 'warm and loving'. More were described as 'good at making decisions and firm'.

Confidence of Parents in Speaking about Religion

65% of the fifteen-year olds and 70% of the seventeen-year olds saw their mothers as 'very sure' or 'pretty sure' when speaking about religion. Approximately 53% of fathers were seen in the same way. Almost 30% of the fathers and 18% of the mothers never spoke of religion to their children.

The answers to the written questions reflect those of the interview. Only a minority of the fifteen- and seventeen-year olds did not see themselves as 'close' to their parents. A higher number of both age-groups saw themselves as 'very close' or 'somewhat close' to their mothers than to their fathers. More mothers than fathers were described as 'warm and loving' and more fathers were seen as 'good at making decisions and firm'. When confidence in speaking about religion was considered, more mothers than fathers were described as 'sure' or 'pretty sure'.

OTHER STUDIES CONCERNING THE INFLUENCE OF PARENTS

Studies[2] dealing with the influence of parents on the attitudes of adolescents have led to the conclusion that adolescents whose attitudes were favourable towards their parents and other adults were more likely to identify with parental and adult values. The life-style of young people was seen to be shaped significantly by the degree to which parents' religious, political and social values were seen as relevant to the young. American studies[3] of the religious development of young people have shown that parents' attitudes to religion were a major factor influencing the religiousness of youth. They found that adolescents with parents described as 'affectionate' and 'supportive' were consistently more positive towards religion, provided the parents were also practising their religion. When young people left the Church or ceased to practise poor relationship within the home and a low level of religious practice by parents were frequently found to be the cause.

While conflict with the mother was seen in many cases to lead to rejection of the mother's religious values[4] it has also been found that the impact of the father's values is greater than the impact of the mother's values.[5] The religious development of young people was seen to depend on the commitment of parents and the successful transmission of religious values in a family whose climate is free from conflict and rebellion.[6] Religious attitudes and behaviour were seen to develop through the influence of both parents. The father was found to have the greater influence when it came to the young actually committing themselves to these values.[7]

A study of young Australian Catholics[8] showed that the students' happiness at home and sense of acceptance and trust were positively relative to Catholic practice. Where students felt trusted and loved at home, were able to discuss problems with parent(s) and relate to other members of the family, they were more open to be involved in the practice of their faith. Similar work with young English Catholics[9] gives firm evidence of the strong influence of home background on the religious behaviour of senior pupils. The extent to which parents identified with the Church and practised their religion was seen as playing an important role in the religious development of youth. A 1984 profile of church-going youth in England[10] led to the conclusion that the degree of the parents' certainty of belief in God and their religious practices seemed to be the most important factors in the transmission of belief and practice in the next generation.

Work with young people in Northern Ireland[11] led to the conclusion that the degree of the parents' strength of belief in God and their religous practice seemed to be important factors in the transmission of belief and practice to the next generation.

A 1984 report on Irish values[12] indicated that the institution of marriage remains strongly upheld and that there is no sign of a growing generation gap between parents and children. While parents were seen as less strict, the qualities they sought to develop in their children were the traditional ones of good neighbour, hard worker and solid citizen. However, the question was also raised regarding the willingness of Irish parents to take on their share of responsibility for developing children's religious faith and confidence in the Church. 'Among the clearest trends on relations between parents and children is the declining importance attached by parents to developing religious faith, age-group by age-group, and among the more educated and qualified'.[13] While reflecting on his experience with Irish university students, Michael Paul Gallagher[14] noted that he had not come across a fully unbelieving university student who had a good relationship with believing parents. He goes on to explain what he means by 'unbelieving', 'good relationship' and 'believing'. By 'fully unbelieving' he meant someone who seems to have closed the door on God in a permanent fashion; by 'good relationship' he suggested a fairly sustained effort on the part of parents to change their way of communication as their child approached adulthood and by 'believing' he meant parents who had avoided the trap for faith in a married context, that of falling into the rut of non-growth, of remaining at the level of pious but conventional belonging to the Church.

THE FAMILY AND THE SCHOOL

It has been pointed out that the family on its own can no longer fulfil the function of passing on important Christian values. It needs the support of the school and parish. The Catholic school is often described as an extension of the Catholic home. A study of the religious effectiveness of some Australian Catholic high schools[15] emphasised the role of parental religious commitment and the young person's happiness and success in the home in explaining attendance at Mass and reception of the sacraments. It also stressed that the school had an independent role to play. The results of the study showed that the way the pupils saw the school had a significant effect on their religious development. Adolescent faith was shown to be influenced, among other things, by:

  1. the students' opinion of the importance of religious goals for

the school, including the building of an atmosphere of Christian community, providing meaningful liturgical celebrations, teaching religious education at a level comparable to other subjects and integrating it with other subjects and providing an example of dedicated life by lay and religious staff;

2. students' level of satisfaction with current religious education programmes;

3. students' liking for teachers and perception that they teach well;

4. students' view of the actual level of importance attached by the school to liberal education goals.[16]

The replies of some young people in County Cork[17] to questions regarding the way they saw their schools showed that the majority agreed that their schools encouraged the practice of Christian values, gave guidelines for recognising right from wrong, and helped in the development of habits of personal prayer. However, only a small proportion were prepared to say that they accepted the religious goals of their school. It was noted that this finding may point to a need for schools to be more specific about clarifying their religious goals, and to encourage dialogue and discussion. A survey of schools in the south west of Ireland[18] regarding teacher and pupil perception of the school environment revealed that 62% of the pupils, 33% of the teachers, and 16% of the administrators could not agree at all that the schools in question considered the religious and moral training of pupils as the most important element in the curriculum. Gabriel Moran[19] notes that little is said about the family in the school curriculum. He believes that, if we talked about education rather than schooling, the family might loom larger in the consciousness of the school. An interesting definition of religious education is quoted by Moran: 'It is whatever affirms the family while at the same time reminding the family that it is not the final community'.[20] The time has come to ask the question: 'How serious are parents and teachers in seeking a co-operative relationship within education, particularly in relation to the education of young people in the faith?'

The more basic question may be: 'How seriously do parents themselves, the school and the State accept that parents are ":the first and foremost educators of their children"?' In the encyclical on the Christian Family in the Modern World[21] it was clearly stated that the right and duty of parents to educate their children is incapable of being entirely delegated to others or usurped by others. The State and Church were seen to have the obligation to give families all possible aid to enable them to perform their educational role properly. Corresponding to their rights, parents were regarded as having a serious duty to commit themselves totally to a cordial and active relationship with the teachers and school authorities. Accepting that there is a growing level of co-operation between home and school, and accepting the finding of the study of Irish values regarding the need for parents to take up their share of responsibility for developing their children's religious faith, it may be assumed that the co-operation is greater in the purely academic and technical areas of the curriculum than in the area of religious education.

THE FAMILY AND THE CHURCH

In the encyclical on the Christian family it was seen as a matter of urgency that the pastoral care of the family be treated as a real matter of priority. It was also accepted that such pastoral action must be progressive – accompanying the Christian family on its journey through life. The setting up of the Pontifical Council for the Family was seen as a sign of the importance which the wider Catholic Church attributed to the pastoral care of the family and it was noted that institutes exist in a number of dioceses to study the problems of the family. The non-existence of such an institute in Ireland and the lack of an organised plan for the pastoral care of families in Ireland are causes for concern. In considering the general principles behind the development of a youth policy[22] it was noted that the government could take one of two courses – 'a *laissez-faire* course to be followed if no National Youth Policy were adopted, or a planned interventionist course to be followed if a National Youth Policy were implemented. If it is believed that young people can enter adult society without undue difficulty or strain, the first course is the more likely to be taken. However, if it is believed that the needs of our young people are so important and urgent that planned responses are required, it is more likely that a National Youth Policy will be drawn up and developed'. The same can be said of the position of the family in the Church today. If it is believed that the Christian family can by itself cope with the influences of an increasing secular and consumer society, the need for pastoral planning is not there. If, on the other hand, it is recognised that this decade is a particularly crucial one for the future of the Church in Ireland and that the family plays a uniquely important role in the Church, then the need for a more co-ordinated pastoral plan is obvious. Efforts are being made in some parishes and dioceses to meet some of the needs of the family of today. But these efforts need to be better co-ordinated and more comprehensive if they are to be effective. Obviously, such pastoral action would involve the family at each level of development – planning, implementation and review.

It has been asserted that the Church's destiny lies entirely with the family, the house Church. Without adults there cannot be an adult Church. And it may be surmised that people can only become adult Christians, if they encounter other adult Christians. The family and the school will be successful in their role of helping children to develop in their relationship with God if they can point to a wider group of people, to a community who together express their belief in God and try to live accordingly. The Church, in so far as it is organised as a large scale institution, has difficulty in providing such support for the family and school. A sense of Christian community does not automatically exist in large parishes. One of the challenges to the Church in Ireland today is the establishment or revival of Christian communities which reflect the larger Church but which are small enough to allow for identification and involvement. Young people need to be part of communities which strive, however inadequately, to express their love of God and love of each other.

AN EMERGING MESSAGE

1. The emotional climate of the homes of the great majority of the young people involved in the study favoured their religious development.

2. Three things seem to characterise homes in which young people are most positive in their approach to religion: (a) a loving and trusting relationship between parents and between parents and children; (b) the expression by parents of their belief in God in their behaviour, values, attitudes, and general life style; (c) discussion of parents' and childrens' religious belief, attitudes, and other values. The absence of any one of these elements seems to lead to a less positive outcome.

3. While the influence of a loving and caring mother cannot be over-estimated, the influence of the father seems particularly significant where commitment to religious values and beliefs are concerned. It would seem to some extent that religion is 'caught' from and nurtured by the mother and that in many cases it is reflected upon, elaborated and decisions made concerning it in relation to the father. Both parents have a particular role to play, and minimum interest or non-involvement of either has a negative impact on the young person's religious growth.

4. A large proportion of the fathers connected with the study did not talk about religion to their children. If faith is a matter of decision, it may well be that the religion of these fathers has more to do with habit and custom than with personal faith and commitment. Should this be true, it would have implications for the eventual level of religious maturity reached by their children.

5. While the family is the primary source of belief, it can also be the primary source of non-belief. An under-nourished faith may, as Michael Paul Gallagher[23] points out, survive for parents because of the depths of its roots, but it will be communicated to children as something shallow and of little worth. Much of our concern for the future strength of Christianity in Ireland is directed at the next generation. Perhaps it could with greater reason be directed to our generation – to the adults who bear the greatest responsibility within it.

The majority of lay people, it is claimed, 'feel unneeded and unchallenged by the institutional Church. Vast resources of goodwill and fine potential remain untapped. Adults need to be motivated to learn more about their religion. They need to feel that all the talk about the importance of their role as the children's primary educators is not just pious cliche'.[24]

6. The quality of the school environment has been shown to have a direct influence on the Christian development of pupils. This influence, it would seem, is to some extent independent of that of the family and Church. If schools are to be faithful to their task, it would appear that they need to examine critically the values which the staff and administration reflect in their everyday relationships with pupils. Schools are accountable to parents and the wider community, and need to be aware of how they are perceived by their pupils, parents and the Christian community. Active co-operation between parents and teachers within educa-

tion will not take place without leadership, planning and commitment. To be effective, such cooperation will involve witnessing to
common values. What are these values? And what are the practical steps parents and teachers must take in order to proclaim and
to witness to them? Young people, parents and teachers need to
decide what values they want to live out as members of the local
Church. In our day it is necessary to make explicit much of what is
implicit.

7. Both the family and school need to experience the pastoral
care of the wider Christian community. Many parishes, as at
present constituted, are too large and unwieldy to facilitate the
coming together of a number of families in such a way as mutually
to strengthen belief in God and commitment to living the message
of the Gospel. Pastoral planning, at both diocesan and parochial
level, is necessary to facilitate the experience of Christian community. The creation of Christian communities which are part of
the larger Church, but are small enough to promote the identity
and development of the members, would seem to be one of the
most important challenges facing the Church in urban Ireland
today. The future of the Church may very well depend on its
willingness and ability to cope with the challenge to develop
smaller Christian communities within the larger parish structure.

SIX

Towards a Preferential Option for Youth

This chapter will consider some ways in which the Church, as people of God, might respond to the needs of its younger members. While it is realised that many of the suggestions may already be in the process of being carried out as parts of existing programmes in different parts of Ireland, it is also appreciated that a greater level of awaremness is required regarding them at a national level. In his consideration of 'Ireland a Church in Need of Conversion'[1] David Regan emphasises the need to rethink on a national scale what it means to be Christians in Ireland today – to rethink what we are about as Church. We need a greater insight into what it is to be a young Catholic in today's world and a greater understanding of what we, the adult members, can do with youth and for youth.

Section one proposes some of the implications and concerns coming from this study of youth and religion. Section two looks at the young people who were seen as best informed and committed as Christians, and examines the principal influences and supports in their development. Section three attempts to spell out the pastoral challenges posed by the youth of today and the need to move the 'option for youth' into a concrete plan.

1. AREAS OF CONCERN IDENTIFIED IN THE PRESENT STUDY

A. A programme which would provide opportunities for reflection on and articulation of experience, for finding in the Church's teaching, in prayer, in liturgy and symbol, a way of clarifying and interpreting experience.

The answers of the fifteen- and seventeen-year olds suggested a high acceptance of traditional beliefs. However, it was also evident that a considerable proportion of the young people had not begun to personalise their beliefs. While Christ was seen as attractive to young people, many had not reached even a minimum level of commitment to him. There was a lack of religious conviction and commitment among a considerable proportion of both the fifteen- and seventeen-year olds. The religious education of young people cannot be confined to teaching doctrines and celebrating the liturgy, but must involve the creation of experiences which establish a sense of community, enable the young person to be a Christian, to practise Christianity, and which address the young in all areas of their lives. If schools are prepared to see themselves as partners with parents and the parish community in helping young people to become Christians, they must be prepared to cater for the social dimension of religion. At present the majority of schools are mainly concerned with the belief, knowledge and worship aspects of Christianity. But Christian action-reflection has to a large extent been overlooked. Supporting Third World causes and the more local charities by fund-raising is a way of deepening social awareness and responsibility. But young people today need other opportunities to become involved in Christian action and to reflect on their own problems, concerns and aspirations. Practical experiences with elderly, sick, handicapped, or more deprived people, and guidance in reflecting on such experiences in the light of the Gospel, the teaching of the Church and prayer will enable young people to personalise their faith and to develop as Christians.

If our young people are to become Christian by conviction and commitment and not merely Christians by convention, they will need to experience the relevance of Christianity through action and reflection. Such an approach to religious education has begun to take shape in a number of schools, but it will need to become widespread. This will demand a review of the school's commitment to the development of its pupils and a willingness to restructure timetables to make it possible for particular age-groups to spend some time on a regular basis in such activity. It is particularly desirable that as far as possible such activity be parish-based. The reflection can take place in the home and school. The importance of reflection on experience cannot be over-estimated. Psychologists have pointed out that youth need time and opportunities to work out their relationships with others and with the world. Youth is the time for such working-out which can take place only with encouragement and opportunities for reflection. Maturity and growth seem to depend on the ability and time to reflect. Such reflection should also attempt to include other aspects of the young person's life – relations within the home, school and parish. The suggestion that such action-reflection be initiated in the school does not imply that it should not operate at parish level as part of a youth formation programme. The Church as currently constituted concentrates on the school rather than on the parish as the forum for the religious education and formation of youth. A different model of Church would place the responsibility with the parish.

In their 1985 pastoral letter on the Young Church the Irish Catholic bishops[2] recognised the sensitivity of young people to issues of injustice. They pointed out that 'their vision calls us in at least two directions: towards a more active Christian involvement in the struggle for justice and towards a more alert Christian critique of the dehumanising forces within our society'. While the parish, home and school have responsibility for helping young people to become actively involved Christians capable of reflecting on society and offering an alert Christian critique, the school has a unique contribution to make to those areas of religious development. As already said, this *praxis* approach to religious education will demand a re-structuring of the school's programme. Yet such a re-structuring could help young people, in the words of the bishops, to experience the Church 'as a community of the friends of Jesus, those who follow his way, those who are guided by his spirit'.

B. The development of a pastoral plan for youth, which would promote a greater participation in the parish community and its celebrations.

The need for a pastoral plan for youth will be discussed later in the chapter. In this section of the chapter consideration of it is limited to the Mass and the community life of the parish. The answers of the young people to the questions dealing with worship indicate that a growing number of young people do not attend Mass. Lack of knowledge about the Mass and the failure to experience the presence of God at Mass account to some extent for non-attendance. While the solution to the problem is a complex one, demanding the renewal of the whole Christian community, an effort could be made to ensure that during their years at school adolescents have the opportunity to attend a number of Masses in the parish, as well as in the school, which are true celebrations. Assistance in developing an understanding of the sign value of the Mass, which would help adolescents to see beyond the Mass as actually celebrated in an ordinary parish community on a Sunday morning, should be planned for.

In an unpublished study carried out by the author, two hundred and eighty two seventeen- and eighteen-year olds, who are members of a number of Dublin parishes, were asked in the spring of 1985 to suggest steps which could be taken to help young people to find Mass a more meaningful experience. Approximately 70% asked that in every parish there be a special youth liturgy each week, and of those 20% mentioned Saturday evening as the most appropriate time. Over 50% saw the need for the involvement of youth in every Mass, either as readers, ministers of the Eucharist, or in leading the singing. The homily was seen by the majority as the part of the Mass most in need of change. They suggested that it be shortened – limited to one point – that it be addressed to the problems and life of young people or to the actual life experiences of the people of the parish. It was obviously felt very strongly that the homily is used to 'get at' young people, since almost 40% requested that it be used to encourage and not condemn young people.

Reference was also made to the need to help young people in particular and parishioners in general to come to a better understanding of the Mass. The first reading was viewed by many as out of date and irrelevant to life, and many young people expressed the wish that more modern language be used. There was an emphasis on increasing the amount of singing, and mention was made of the need for some priests to be more interested in what was going on. Some young people queried the attitudes towards the Mass of priests who seemed bored and not to enjoy the Mass. There was an appeal for small churches and congregations.

Appreciating the differing needs of a large parish, the majority of young people reiterated their desire for youth liturgies which would be celebrated in a joyful and relaxed way, prepared for by a few moments of explanation and silence, which would permit shared homilies related to Christ and life and, when possible, would be celebrated by younger priests.

A pastoral plan deliberately aimed at facilitating an appreciation of and commitment to the liturgical dimension of the life of faith among adolescents should not be seen as pandering to the young but rather as meeting people where they are and as responding to their developmental needs. The continued lack of such a plan can only lead to a continued decrease in the number of young people attending Mass. Since it can no longer be assumed that the young non-attender of today will become the committed adult attender of tomorrow, it would seem desirable to introduce such a plan, at least in pilot form, as soon as possible.

If adolescents are to develop positive attitudes to the Church, it would seem important that they be given opportunities to identify with adult members of the Christian community, and to contribute practically to the local Church. Direct involvement in suitable activities could lead to a sense of community and could foster an awareness of social justice. A pastoral plan involving the adult members of the parish and specifically designed to facilitate the integration of the young more fully into the Christian community could result in more committed young Catholics.

The group of seventeen- and eighteen-year olds who were asked to make suggestions concerning the Mass were also requested to consider the following two questions: 'Young people are members of the parish community. What would you like to be able to do for your parish? What can the parish do to involve young people in the life of the parishes?'

Approximately 55% said they would like to do something worthwhile for elderly, sick and deprived people. There was particular understanding of and sympathy for the position of elderly and a desire to assure them that the majority of young people were concerned about them. There was also a strong desire to be involved in every level of the parish life, including the parish council. As with the Mass, a large proportion of the group (47%) felt that young people needed to feel welcome and accepted. It is obvious that many young people experienced a certain rejection and neglect. It is apparent also that they would like to be allowed to contribute to their parish apart from being asked to sell tickets. There was a recognition that youth must be prepared to give and take, and that adults need help to be more positive in their attitudes to youth.

A sense of identification with other young people was also strong. Many expressed the desire to promote the coming together of youth in order to create a sense of purpose and hope. The unemployed were frequently spoken of, and the need to provide a parish centre for them was often mentioned. A few young people spoke of the need to build a community of trust and care and appreciated that the larger parish would need to contain a number of such communities.

These young people also felt that they would like to be involved in the running of various youth clubs and organisations, also in the summer project for children. While a large proportion wished to be associated with the provision of sport facilities, a smaller but significant group wanted to contribute to their parish as members of a folk group or a liturgy group. There was an awareness that the parish needed to show concern for the total individual and not just 'for his soul'. These seventeen- and eighteen-year olds wanted to be part of a parish which showed practical concern for elderly, sick or deprived people, was involved in doing something concrete for the unemployed, which welcomed youth and promoted friendship among them. A small minority did not want to do anything for their parish or their parish to do anything for them.

When reflecting on what their parish could do to involve young people in its life, the majority put an emphasis on offering youth a sense of hope and attempting to do something for the unemployed. The provision of youth centres, sports facilities, youth programmes was also seen to be concern of the parish. There were comprehensive expectations regarding the parish, and the genuineness of the Church's interest in youth was seen in relation to the effort it made to meet the various needs of youth. A statement of one young man summed up the attitude: 'I do not want to belong to a parish that is glad to see me in the bench on Sunday and has no interest in me for the rest of the week'. The desire to be members of the parish committees, to run their own youth organisations and to be among the leaders of the Sunday liturgy was also expressed by a large number. Almost 20% asked that 'interesting talks be organised by and for youth, and that young people have an opportunity to mix with priests and older adults'. A parish youth committee was seen as an essential by almost 18% in order for the opinions of young people to be expressed, heard and implemented. Youth programmes were divided into leisure activities and various types of training programmes. There was also a request that youth be given responsibility for caring for specific groups within the parish, e.g., the elderly, and children during school holidays. A small number wanted to be part of an effort to develop pride in the parish and to clean up the area.

C. An investigation into the learning problems posed by the way in which important beliefs are doctrinally expressed

The findings of the present study regarding knowledge and belief indicate that an investigation needs to be carried out regarding the learning problems posed by the way important beliefs are formulated. The Irish Report of the European Value Systems Study[3] also showed that the Church in Ireland 'has problems of straightforward evangelisation (clearing up confusion about who God is, for example)'. Educators in other areas of the school curriculum are coming to grips with the learning problems associated with their disciplines. While a similar effort by religious educators has already begun, much more needs to be accomplished if there is to be a greater understanding of the learning problems posed by some doctrines regarded as basic religious truths. 'Looking at her script, rather than at her audience the Church ran the risk of preaching, not to our generation, but to one which has been dead for hundreds of years'.[4] Today's generation need to hear the message of the Gospel explained in ways which promote meaning, not obscure it.

'Evangelisation will lose much of its power and efficiency if it does not take into consideration the people to whom it is addressed; if it does not make use of their language, their signs and their symbols; if it does not offer an answer to the questions which are relevant to them; if, in a word, it does not reach and influence their ways of life'.[5]

The problem is more than the choice of words used to express a particular religious truth. The nature of some truths is such that understanding of them can only be achieved by relatively mature minds. While it is accepted that a fuller understanding of some religious truths is dependent among other things on prayer, study and motivation, it is also obvious that they can pose particular difficulties for the maturing intelligence of an adolescent. Because of this, they can be dismissed as irrelevant to life.

The Catholic bishops in Ireland have spoken of young people falling victims to inadequate perceptions of a deep reality.[6] It was also noted that the inarticulate and incoherent responses of many young people concerning basic matters of faith suggested that, whatever processes had been used to help them understand the basis of Christian understanding, 'not much of that teaching "stuck" with them'.[7] A study of the actual learning problems associated with the doctrinal expression of some basic religious truths could lead to insight regarding the most appropriate phase of development at which the doctrines should be introduced to the pupils. Because of the relative ease and success with which they have arrived at their own understanding many priests and other adult Christians may fail to appreciate the significance and implication of the learning problem posed by the doctrinal expression of some basic religious truths for today's young people. This type of investigation could profitably be undertaken by colleges preparing professional religious educators, Catholic communication centres, and by clerical students.

D. Adult religious education

The need for continued religious education among adults is obvious. The need is made clear both by the low level of religious knowledge and understanding of the majority of the respondents and because of the significant role played by parents in the religious development of children. As already pointed out in this book, the real challenge to the Church of the future is not the children but the adults.

E. A further longer term study of young people's religion

The finding that at the age of fifteen some young people had already ceased to practise their religion and were experiencing doubts about basic Christian beliefs indicates a need to undertake a further study beginning with a younger age-group (preferably with pupils in their final year of primary school education). Such a study could follow the religious development of a representative group of children through the years of adolescence and into early adulthood. It would facilitate a more accurate identification of growth or regression in various aspects of religious knowledge, beliefs, practice and commitment. It would also lead to a deeper insight into the developmental needs and potential of young people, and enable the adult members of the Christian community to respond in a manner which could more effectively encourage development and prevent regression. Such a study could also throw light on the significance of the roles of family, school and parish community in facilitating the faith development of the young at particular periods in their lives. A study of this kind could easily be carried out by one of the colleges concerned with the professional preparation of religious educators.

2. THE BETTER INFORMED AND COMMITTED YOUNG CATHOLICS:
WHAT CAN BE LEARNED FROM THEIR RESPONSES AND BACKGROUND

Parents frequently ask the question, 'How can we help our children to become good Christians?' This section of the chapter looks at some of the most informed and committed young Catholics of today, and sees how they differ from their more negative counterparts. The qualities of the more positive adolescent may offer guidelines to parents, teachers and others concerning the steps that can be taken to help young people develop in their faith.

Different statistical techniques were used to analyse the vast amount of material used in the research. Approximately one hundred and twenty pieces of information were available on each of the two thousand and four hundred young people involved. As a result of these analyses a number of factors emerged which seemed, at least to some extent, to account for the differences in the responses of the young people who participated in the study.

Adolescents who scored more highly in relation to these factors were seen to be more positive in relation to religion, while those who achieved lower scores emerged as more negative.

The following were the more significant common factors among the the committed fifteen-year olds:

1. They had a basic level of knowledge and could articulate this knowledge. They had a certain religious articulateness

2. They saw religious beliefs and practice as important for themselves and others.

3. They had a satisfactory relationship with their parents.

4. They had a positive experience of the Church as a teaching community.

These young people had a level of awareness about themselves – what they hoped to be, the role of religion in helping them to become the type of person they hoped to be, the difficulties they experienced in being a Catholic and the important things they had learned about religion. They had a relatively clear idea of what it was to be a Christian and could express their opinion of what the Church was doing and should be doing for youth. The obligation to work for social justice was also something they could reflect upon. They also had a reasonably good level of knowledge of basic Catholic beliefs and could give adequate explanations to an enquiring non-Catholic friend of what God, Jesus, the Holy Spirit, the Church, Mass, sacraments and being a Christian meant to

Catholics. These young people had reflected on their faith and could speak about it in a reasonably clear way. They had also achieved a level of personalisation regarding basic beliefs – seeing them as important for themselves and for others. Mass, Communion, Confession, and prayer were seen as relevant to life; religious principles operated at home and in other activities. God was experienced as important in times of joy and sorrow.

These young people seem to come from homes and communities where being a Catholic was important for both children and adults. While closeness to mother and the closeness of parents characterised the families of those young people, closeness to father and a favourable perception of him were particularly significant. Both parents spoke about religion and what it meant to them. They were not theologians, and their children did not expect them to be such. However, they know who and what they believed in, and could speak about their faith. Their ordinary every-day conduct expressed an effort to live their convictions. These positive young people seem to have been in contact with parents and other adults whose lives witnessed to Christian values. They also had helpful experiences of the Church as a teaching community, having found religious lessons relevant and priests and teachers of religion understanding of the problems of young people.

Obviously, there are many degrees of being positive. A large proportion of the young people, who had a basic knowledge of religious beliefs and could articulate this knowledge, did so in a less adequate manner than their more positive peers. The more negative of the fifteen-year olds had difficulty in articulating their views and had relatively little knowledge about religious beliefs. They did not seem to have experienced religion as important for themselves or others. The homes of many of them were lacking in warmth, and religion was rarely mentioned by either parent. Those young people found it difficult to identify anything in their parents' way of living which indicated that religion played a significant role in their lives. These young people also seemed to have negative experiences of the Church as a teaching community. Priests, teachers of religion, and religion classes were not viewed as helpful.

The significant common factors that identified the committed seventeen-year olds can be listed:

1. They saw religious belief and action as personally important.
2. They had a basic knowledge of religion and were able to articulate it.
3. They had a satisfactory relationship with their parents.
4. They had a positive experience of the Church as a teaching community.
5. They showed an adequate level of moral reasoning and action.
6. They were capable of moral sensitivity.
7. They indicated a sense of solidarity with other Christians.
8. They gave evidence of commitment above the minimum in relation to worship and action.

While these positive seventeen-year olds saw religion as important for others, there was more emphasis than at fifteen on its personal significance. Jesus was seen in relation to their own lives, and religion was seen as contributing to their development and welfare. Mass, Confession and prayer as well as religious principles were viewed as relevant to life and God was found to be important in moments of joy and sorrow. Being a Catholic was perceived as meaningful for self and for others. These seventeen-year olds also had a basic knowledge of important religious beliefs. This knowledge extended over a greater range of beliefs than was the case with the fifteen-year olds. As with the positive fifteen-year old, there was an ability to articulate views and beliefs. These seventeen-year olds had a confidence in expressing their beliefs and could give satisfactory explanations of them.

The home situation and the perception of the Church as a teaching community seemed similar to those of the fifteen-year olds. Moral reasoning and action appeared to be important elements in the religion of the committed seventeen-year olds. They knew what to do in specific situations and were aware of their motivation for acting in a particular way. In addition, there was a sensitivity to the more vulnerable members of society and a sense of solidarity with others who showed that their religion was important. The more committed seventeen-year olds also showed a degree of commitment which could be described as above the minimum. They had a greater appreciation of the missionary role and activity of the Church; they prayed, attended Mass, Communion and Confession more frequently than the majority of their peers. They also read religious material.

Certain common factors also appeared among the more negative seventeen-year olds:

1. They did not feel religious beliefs and practice meant much to them.

2. They had difficulty in articulating their beliefs, and their religious knowledge was inadequate

3. Their homes would seem to provide less love, trust and acceptance than those of their more positive peers.

4. The Church as a teaching community had not been experienced in a helpful way.

5. Moral reasoning and action were less developed, and there was less moral sensitivity regarding people in vulnerable positions.

6. There was little evidence of a sense of solidarity with other Christians.

Guidelines

It would seem that the qualities which characterise the more positive fifteen- and seventeen-year olds offer insights regarding the religious growth of young people. The following guidelines have been derived from them. Obviously, these guidelines are not exhaustive and need to be concretised to suit particular situations. However, a concerted attempt to implement them by parents, clergy and teachers could but contribute to young people's development as Christians.

1. Help young people to acquire a basic knowledge of the most important Christian beliefs, to personalise this knowledge and to develop confidence in their ability to speak about what they believe.

2. Enable young people to develop a relationship with Christ which would make being a Christian personally meaningful and would lead to the recognition of the significance of personal and community worship and service.

3. Support parents in their efforts to build loving and supportive relationships, to grow in their own faith, to dialogue about it with their children (listening to their children and being prepared to speak of their own convictions), and to live this faith as best as they can in their daily lives, knowing that action speaks louder than words.

4. Find ways of making it possible for young people to come in contact with their committed peers and with understanding adults

at parish level, with whom they can share their difficulties and hopes.

5. Assist the Church as a teaching community to be more effective in meeting the needs of youth.

6. Show youth that the local Christian community makes an effort to live its values, particularly in relation to the disadvantaged and marginalised, and welcomes their participation in such efforts.

7. Provide opportunities which enable young people to experience Christianity at a deeper level offering a vision, however partial, of what it means to follow Christ.

3. THE PASTORAL CHALLENGE OF YOUTH TODAY

Such an approach to the religious development of children and young people would largely depend on the degree to which significant adults were aware of what it means to be a young person in the Church of today. Much would also depend upon the adult's understanding of what it is to be a Christian today, belonging to the Church of today. When writing or talking about the Church in Ireland, what comes to the mind of the majority of the Irish people would probably be the institutional Church, which is largely associated with the bishops and clergy. While many people have been taught that the Church is the people of God, they would claim that such a Church is not a reality as far as they are concerned. At best it is only coming into being in Ireland. It is easier to place all the blame for the failures of the Church on the bishops and clergy than to face the challenge of being a member of the people of God, accepting responsibility for the rethinking that is needed. (When an unqualified reference is made to the Church in this section it is the institutional Church which is under consideration).

Before we the Church as the people of God can begin to respond in any depth to the needs of youth, we need to envision what we are about. We also need to be committed to articulating this vision and in some ways at least to think of this vision in terms of goals towards which to work. While our vision will always exceed our power to achieve it, it must be capable of being expressed, however inadequately, in word and action. The Church which can respond to the needs of youth is the Church as people of God. Only such a Church will have the necessary human resources. Many priests find themselves so busy with the sacramental ministry and the administration of parishes that they simply do not have time to minister to the young in a way which reaches the majority of young people in their parish.

With the active involvement of young people and committed adult members much could be achieved. It has been argued that we cannot have a pastoral plan for youth until we have a pastoral plan for the wider Church community. The latter would certainly enhance the former. However, can we in Ireland, with half our population under the age of twenty five, justify such a delay? Pastoral planning for youth can always be modified in the light of more comprehensive planning. This may not be desirable, but it may be necessary.

The Latin American bishops at their Conference in Puebla declared a preferential option for the poor and for the young. The goal of such an option was 'to introduce young people to the living Christ, as the one and only Saviour, so that they will be evangelised, and evangelise in return, so that they in loving response to Christ, will contribute to the integrant liberation of the human being and society by leading a life of communion and participation'.[8]

These bishops sought to elaborate a pastoral effort for young people which would take into account their social reality, foster the growth and deepening of faith for the sake of communion with God and their neighbour, enable them to mature as lay person, priest or religious, offer them the resources for becoming agents of change, and enable them to participate actively and effectively in the Church community, and in the transformation of society. It has been noted that throughout the Church in general 'the option for the young has in general been passed over in total silence'.[9] Many young people in Ireland would be justified in describing the option for youth as the forgotten option. It has been said that 'unfortunately the only significant action with, for and on behalf of youth is taking place at the fringes of the Church, among isolated priests, religious and laity'.[10] While recognising that the Church has invested considerable resources in the education of youth, it is becoming more obvious that the character of schools is changing. In the pluralist state which Ireland is becoming the Church may find that more of its resources must be channelled into pastoral action on behalf of youth at parish level. It has been argued that 'young people are "mission territory" in Ireland today, not because they are missing Mass and Confession, but because they are victims of a society that is increasingly excluding them from all that is necessary to live a full human life. In the context of Ireland today the Church's option for the poor must include an option for the young'.[11] An understanding of the Church as a community of people of God, or of the Church as sign symbolising the mission of Jesus would demand that the Church in Ireland makes its option for the young more explicit. The Church in Ireland has always been at the service of youth, its huge investment in education being one example of its interest and commitment. But this service must take on a radical new form if it is to be in touch with the implications of pluralism and consumerism, with nationalism and unemployment.

The need 'to begin to devise a pastoral strategy which will build community (i.e., small communities) and enable participation of all who belong to it' was identified as one of the main recommendations for action in an analysis of ministry in the Church as a context for youth ministry.[12] It was also recognised that a whole new attitude is needed by people and leaders to initiate such a pastoral strategy. The time has come for the Church to express its service of young people in an option for youth which is articulated and made concrete in a pastoral plan.

While the Church in Ireland needs to articulate its policy or pastoral plan for youth, it may be unable to do so until it develops and articulates its understanding of Church. In talking about youth ministry, one of the Church leaders, Bishop Donal Murray, stated:

> Youth ministry, therefore, is not simply the ministry of adults to young people, nor simply the ministry of young people to each other; it is a way of talking about being the Church, engaged in the never-ending task of enabling the Gospel to take flesh in the mentality and characteristics of the new generation.[13]

Ministry may be understood as the activity of one group in relation to another in order to facilitate their full and active involvement as followers of Christ, in the Church as the community of the people of God. If youth ministry is a way of talking about the Church, and if youth themselves play such a significant role in it, then young people need help to become 'the first apostles of the young, in direct contact with them, exercising the apostolate – by themselves, among themselves, taking into account their social environment'.[14] It has been pointed out that there are over six hundred thousand young people in Ireland, and that little is being done to help them to minister to one another.[15] The documents of the Second Vatican Council outline the type of training needed: 'Training for the apostolate cannot consist of theoretical teaching alone; on that account there is need, right from the start to learn to see all things in the light of faith, to judge and act always in its light, and in that manner, to enter actively into the service of the Church'.[16] Until the more recent past the Church in Ireland may not have needed to take youth ministry and preparation for the lay apostolates seriously. 'To be a forward looking Church we have to use pastoral and not dogmatic methods. When we adopt a pastoral approach we get a better sense of time and place – these are the very co-ordinates of pastoral effort – and we are better able to countenance change'.[17] A new awareness of time and place will create the sense of urgency and hope necessary to respond to the fast-changing Irish society and the more enriched understanding of the Church. We must be fully aware of the positive and the negative in the Ireland of today and respond accordingly. One such response could take the form of a pastoral plan for youth, which would attempt to integrate the roles of parent, parish, school and young people, and which would involve their representatives in its development, implementation and evaluation. And why? Because 'the vision of our ministry begins with our vision of Jesus Christ. The aim of ministry is to put people not only in touch but also in communion with Jesus Christ'.[18]

While the Church in Ireland does not seem to have a preferential option for youth and only recently has explicitly expressed a commitment to facilitate their full participation in the life of the Church, it has in a limited way attempted to answer the needs of the young today. The formation of the National Committee of Priest Youth Directors and the association of four bishops with their work is one such response. While reflecting on the 'Emerging Church' Michael Lioston notes:

> If I was writing in 1974 on the subject of young people and the Church, I might have started with a list of negatives and then announced 'shoulds'. Now in 1983, I think the first reality is that in the midst of all the negative aspects, there is a lot of Church life that is fresh and growing, as young people become aware of themselves and their bonds with each other in the

Body of Christ. The Holy Spirit is building a Young Church among us, an *Eaglais Óg*. [19]

Through the pioneering efforts of a number of priests, religious and laity, including young people themselves, a growing proportion of Irish youth are living the life of the Church through movements and centres such as the Y.C.W, Y.C.S., Impact, *Muintearas Íosa, Teach Bríde*, Discovery, *Fáilte*.

An account[20] of these developments presents an encouraging and practical description of what has taken place since the mid 1970s. But while it was agreed that there has always been an interest in the needs of young people in our history,,the question was asked: 'Could we describe such an interest in youth as an option for youth by the Church as a whole?' In contrast to the general scene there is a growing number of people who regard the following framework as a basic description of what they are about:

We must start with the mission of Christ to carry out the
Father's plan to bring people

from	*to*
isolation	community
insignificance	recognition
materialism	spiritual values
lack of meaning	truth
all that opposes	freedom
guilt	reconciliation
death	life of the children of God. [21]

One of the theories put forward to account for the relative lack of response of the Church to youth in the present situation is the lack of agreement as a description of what is happening or not happening. Recognising that in each parish there are the committed, the middle-of-the-road, and the marginalised, a proposal was put forward regarding a locally based ministry for the pastoral care of youth. Allowing for a degree of overlap, it was suggested that a ministry of formation be provided for the committed, a ministry of friendship for the middle-of-the-road, and a ministry of service for the marginalised. [22]

While a promising beginning has been made in relation to a small proportion of our young people, a particular problem has been identified regarding them. 'It is one thing to offer an experience of Church as friendship, community, a place of free expression, prayer, reconciliation, service, etc., and another thing to sustain a community that lives these values.'[23] However, a beginning has been made and there is sufficient experience of actual work by, with and for youth to provide some important material for the development of a preliminary pastoral plan for youth. In the meantime and perhaps for all time, 'the transformation of Church and society in Ireland, if it is going to happen at all, will be the fruits of a lot of struggles, a lot of initiatives, a lot of failures by small groups of very ordinary fallible, vulnerable people on the ground'.[24]

The letter of the bishops of Ireland to all concerned with the pastoral care of youth[25] expresses warm appreciation of the work of these small groups of people. It expresses a sincere desire to listen to young people, a recognition of their contribution to the life of the Church, and a warm clear understanding of the significance of the work of youth with youth and for youth. There is an openness to re-thinking our inherited Christianity and a willingness to work with youth 'in building on the foundations of the past but in ways that are faithful to the present and future'. The letter also offers a vision of God, Christ and the Church which cannot but inspire. But if these values and ideals are not expressed, at least to some extent, in action this pastoral will become just another letter from the bishops. A possible basis for a pastoral plan for youth is provided in the outline of the challenges facing the Church today. The key challenge is seen as 'the struggle to live true to our humanity now and to Christ now'. The challenges for the Church were seen as coming from Christ and the Gospel. And the bishops saw the need to help young people to face these challenges:

> to face the question of Christ, 'Who do you say I am?'
> to come and see what faith might be,
> to be open to accept forgiveness,
> to recognise him in the breaking of bread,
> to watch and pray to be saved from deceptions,
> to find and follow his way in the world of today,
> to let go of self and give oneself for others,
> to learn to love the 'least' of people, even our enemies,
> to receive his Spirit within the community,
> to become bearers of a living Gospel that can heal the world.

As said in the letter, what has been written will be fruitless if it does not lead to action and renewal that involves the young people. The bishops as well as young people themselves, families, schools anmd parishes have a responsibility to translate words into action. And as bishops they have a particular leadership role to play in facilitating the development of diocesan or regional pastoral plans for youth which can be modified and implemented at parish level. If the bishops in partnership with young people, their parents, teachers, youth workers and clergy could develop a pilot pastoral plan for youth, the challenge of today will be in the process of being met.

Notes

INTRODUCTION
1. D. Murray, *The Future of the Faith*, Veritas, Dublin, 1985, p. 26.
2. *ibid.*
3. Catholic Bishops of Ireland, *The Young Church: God's Gift in Your Care*, Veritas, Dublin, 1985.
4. A. Breslin and J. Weafer, *Religious Beliefs, Practice and Moral Attitudes*, Maynooth, Council for Research and Development, 1985, p. 146.
5. M. Nic Ghiolla Phádraig, 'Religion in Ireland - Preliminary Analysis', *Social Studies*, Vol. 5, No. 2 Summer 1976, pp. 113-180
6. A. Breslin, J. Weafer, *op. cit.*, p. 144.
7. M. P. Hornsby Smith, *Catholic Education*, Sheed and Ward, London, 1978.
8. J. W. Fowler, *Stages of Faith*, Harper and Row, New York, 1981.

ONE: YOUNG BELIEVERS
1. M. P. Hornsby Smith, *Catholic Education*, Sheed and Ward, London, 1978.
2. *ibid.*
3. Duke and Whitton, Discussion Paper on the Study of Young People's Beliefs, General Synod Board of Education, 1977.
4. K. E. Hyde, *Religious Learning in Adolescents*, Oliver and Boyd, London, 1965.
5. F. B. Turner, 'General Cognitive Ability and Religious Attitudes in Two School Systems', *British Journal of Religious Education*, Autumn 1979.
6. M. Fogarty, L. Ryan, J. Lee, *Irish Values and Attitudes: The Irish Report of the European Value Systems Study*, Dominican Publications, Dublin, 1984.
7. A. Breslin, J. Weafer, *A Survey of Senior Students' Attitudes Towards Religion, Morality, Education*, Council for Research and Development, Maynooth, 1982.
8. M. Fogarty, L. Ryan, J. Lee, *op. cit.*, p. 91.
9. *ibid.* p. 93.

TWO: YOUNG WORSHIPPERS
1. R. Potvin, D. R. Hoge, H. M. Nelson, *Religion and American Youth*, United States Catholic Conference, 1976.
2. Duke and Whitton, Discussion Paper on the Study of Young People's Beliefs, General Synod Board of Education, 1977.
3. M. P. Hornsby Smith, *Catholic Education*. Sheed and Ward, London, 1978.
4. L. J. Francis, *Teenagers and the Church: A Profile of Church-going Youth in the 1908s*, Collins, London, 1984.
5. M. Nic Ghiolla Phádraig, 'Religion in Ireland - Preliminary Analysis', *Social Studies*, Vol. 5 No. 2 (1976) pp. 113-180.
6. A. Breslin, J. Weafer, *A Survey of Senior Students' Attitudes Towards*

Religion, Morality and Education, Council for Research and Development, Maynooth, 1982.

7. M. P. Gallagher, *Help My Unbelief,* Veritas, Dublin, 1984, p. 42.

THREE: THE YOUNG CHURCH MEMBER

1. R. Potovin and D. R. Hoge, *Religon and American Youth 1976,* U. S. Catholic Conference, 1976.

2. L. J. Francis, *Teenagers and the Church,* Collins, London, 1984.

3. M. P. Hornsby Smith, *Catholic Education,* Sheed and Ward, London, 1978.

4. J. McKenna, 'A Survey among 17- to 19-year old School Leavers, 1983, to Evaluate their Concept of Christ and of their Relationship to Him', Unpublished Study, Irish School of Ecumenics.

5. M. Fogarty, L. Ryan, J. Lee, *Irish Values and Attitudes: The Irish Report of the European Value Systems Survey,* Dominican Publications, Dublin, 1984.

FOUR: THE YOUNG CATHOLIC IN THE WORLD

1. A. M. Greeley, W. C. McCready, K. McCourt, *Catholic Schools in a Declining Church,* Sheed and Ward, London, 1976 p. 288.

2. M. Nic Ghiolla Phádraig, 'Religion in Ireland - Preliminary Analysis', *Social Studies,* Vol. 5, No. 2 (Summer 1976), pp. 113-180.

3. T. Inglis, *Students and Religion: Survey of Religious Practice, Attitudes and Beliefs of Irish University Students,* Council for Research and Development, Maynooth, 1976.

4. Catholic Bishops of Ireland, *The Work of Justice,* Veritas, Dublin, 1977, p. 18.

5. A Breslin, J. Weafer, *A Survey of Senior Students' Attitudes Towards Religion, Morality and Education,* Council for Research and Development, Maynooth, 1982.

6. A. Breslin, 'Are Religious Persons Prejudiced?', *The Furrow,* February 1985.

7. L. J. Francis, *Teenagers and the Church,* Collins, London, 1984.

8. M. Nic Ghiolla Phádraig, 'Roman Catholics in England, Wales, and Ireland – Surveys compared', *Doctrine and Life,* December 1981.

9. P. J. Philibert, J. P. O'Connor, 'Adolescent Religious Socialisation: A Study of Goal Priorities – According to Parents and Religious Educators', *Review of Religious Research,* Vol. 23, No. 3, March 1982.

10. C. Daly, 'The Poor You Have Always with You', *The Furrow,* February 1985.

11. P. S. Fahy, 'The Religious Effectiveness of Some Australian High Schools', *Word in Life,* August 1980.

12. J. H. Westerhoff, *Will Our Children Have Faith?,* Seabury Press, p. 105.

13. *ibid.* p. 108.

14. *ibid.*

15. J. McKenna, 'A Survey Among 17- to 19-year old School Leavers to Evaluate Their Concept of Christ and Their Relationship with Him', Unpublished Study, Irish School of Ecumenics.

16. W. Kay, 'Christ and Christianity for Children Today', *Lumen Vitae,* Vol. XXVIII, 1972, pp. 464-488.

17. *ibid.* p. 488.

FIVE: YOUNG CATHOLICS AND THEIR FAMILIES

1. J. W. Fowler, *Stages of Faith,* Harper and Row, New York, 1981.

2. D. F. Duncan, 'Measuring the Generation Gap: Attitudes Towards Parents and Other Adults', *Adolesence,* No. 13, 1978, pp. 77-81.

3. R. Potvin, D. R. Hoge, H. M. Nelson, *Religion and American Youth,* Publication Office U.S. Catholic Conference, 1976.

4. J. W. Kotre, *The View from the Border,* Aldine G. Atherton, 1971.

5. L. Longman, R. L. Black, I. Cunningham, 'Counter Cultural Values at a Catholic University', *Social Problems* 20 (Spring 1973), pp. 521-532.

6. D. R. Hoge, G. Petrillo, 'Determinants of Church Participation among High School Youth', *Journal* 17, No. 4, 1978, pp. 359-379.

7. A. M. Greeley, W. C. McCready, 'Socialisation and the Persistance of Religion', *Concilium,* January 1973, pp. 58-68.

8. P. S. Fahy, 'The Religious Effectiveness of Some Australian High Schools', *Word in Life,* August 1980.

9. M. P. Hornsby Smith, *Catholic Education,* Sheed and Ward, London, 1980.

10. L. J. Francis, *Teenagers and the Church: A Profile of Church Going Youth in the 1980s,* Collins, London, 1984.

11. J. E. Greer, 'Religious Belief and Church Attendance of Sixth Form Pupils and Their Parents', *Irish Journal of Education,* Vol. 2, 1971, pp. 48-106.

12. M. Fogarty, L. Ryan, J. Lee, *Irish Values and Attitudes: Irish Report of the European Values Systems Study,* Dominican Publications, Dublin, 1984.

13. *ibid.* p. 93.

14. M. P. Gallagher, *Help My Unbelief,* Veritas, Dublin, 1984.

15. P. S. Fahy, *op. cit.*

16. *ibid.*

17. A. Breslin, J. Weafer, *A Survey of Senior Students' Attitudes Towards Religion, Morality, Education,* Council for Research and Development, Maynooth, 1982.

18. E. O'Sullivan, 'Perceptions of Educational Environment in South West Ireland', Unpublished Ph.D. Study, Ann Arbor.

19. G. Moran, *Religious Education Development,* Winston Press, 1983.

20. S. Callahan, 'Family Religious Education', *Living Light,* II, Summer 1974, pp. 235-264.

21. Pope John Paul II, *The Christian Family in the Modern World,* Catholic Truth Society, London, 1981.

22. National Youth Policy Committee, *Final Report,* Government Publications, Dublin, 1984.

23. M. P. Gallagher, *op. cit.*

24. A. Macnamara, *The Furrow,* January 1985, p. 57.

SIX: TOWARDS A PREFERENTIAL OPTION FOR YOUTH

1. D. Regan, 'Ireland, A Church in Need of Conversion', *Doctrine and Life,* April 1985, p. 202.

2. Catholic Bishops of Ireland, *The Young Church: God's Gift in Your Care,* Veritas, Dublin, 1985, p. 10.

3. M. Fogarty, L. Ryan, J. Lee, *Irish Values and Attitudes: The Irish Report of the European Value Systems Study,* Dominican Publications. 1984, p. 93.

4. D. Regan, *art. cit.* p. 204.

5. Pope Paul VI, 'Evangelii Nuntiandi' (par. 63) in *Evangelisation Today,* Dominican Publications, Dublin, 1977.

6. Catholic Bishops of Ireland, *op. cit.,* p. 15.

7. M. Clarke, M. Howlett and J. McDermott, *Mustard Seeds,* Veritas, Dublin, p. 5.

8. J. Eagleson, P. Scharpar (edd.), *Puebla and Beyond,* Orbis, Maryknoll, 1980, p. 267.

9. Sacred Congregation for the Doctrine of the Faith, *Instruction on Certain Aspects of the Theology of Liberation,* Vatican City Press, 1984, p. 16.

10. S. Claffey, 'Exclusion: Young People and the Church – an Overview', *Resource,* Spring 1985, p. 4.

11. *ibid.*

12. M. Clarke, M. Howlett and J. McDermott, *op. cit.,* p. 28.

13. D. Murray, 'Youth Ministry', in *Dublin Diocesan Bulletin,* November 1982, p. 12.

14. Pope Paul VI, *op. cit.,* par. 72.

15. M. Kennedy, 'Towards a Young Adult Ministry', *Intercom,* October 1984.

16. A. Flannery, (ed.), *Vatican II: Conciliar and Post-Conciliar Documents,* Dominican Publications, Dublin, p. 794.

17. D. Regan, *art. cit.,* p. 203.

18. B. Comiskey, 'The Role of Priest in the Ministry of Young People', Unpublished Paper.

19. M. Lioston, 'The Emerging Church', *Resource,* Vol. 2 No. 1, (Spring 1983), p. 22.

20. M. Clarke, M. Howlett and J. McDermott, *op. cit.,* p. 27.

21. M. Liostan, *art. cit.,* p. 21.

22. M. Kennedy, *art. cit.*

23. M. Liostan, *art. cit.,* p. 18.

24. M. Kennedy, 'Leader Guide', *Resource,* Vol. 2, No. 1 (Spring 1983), p. 18.

25. Catholic Bishops of Ireland, *op. cit.*